Above Only

And Anxious For Nothing!

Common $ense Guidelines For Managing Your Finances

Joseph C. Brown

Powerful wealth-building principles for getting out of debt, reducing taxes, eliminating anxiety about money, getting organized, starting a business, planning for retirement, and more.

Dedicated to my dearly loved family.

PLEASE READ: We have made every effort to provide useful and accurate information and techniques on personal financial management and how to gain financial fitness and freedom. Neither the publisher nor author makes any warranties concerning the information in this book, or the use to which it is put. All biblical quotations in this book are from the King James and New King James versions of the *Holy Bible*.

Library of Congress Control Number: 2002090639

ISBN 0-9718623-0-3

Copyright © 2002 Joseph C. Brown and Above Only Media. All rights reserved. No part of this publication may be reproduced, stored in a retrieval system, or transmitted, in any form or by any means, electronic, mechanical, photocopying, recording, or otherwise, without the prior written consent of the author or publisher.

First printing March 2002

Printed in the United States of America
by Signature Book Printing, Inc. Gaithersburg, MD.

If your local bookstore is out of this title, ask them to order it for you. You can also order directly from the publisher at the address below or online at www.aboveonlymedia.com.

Above Only Media
P.O. Box 32421
Baltimore, MD. 21282-2421

TABLE OF CONTENTS

PREFACE 3

INTRODUCTION 7

WHY AND WHERE TO START 11

ESTABLISH YOUR GOALS 23

TRACK YOUR EXPENSES 31

CUT EXPENSES AND INCREASE INCOME 37

WHAT TO DO WITH THE INCREASED INCOME 55

SEVEN SECRETS "THEY" DON'T WANT YOU TO KNOW 63

TWELVE THINGS I WISH I HAD KNOWN TWENTY YEARS AGO 83

WHERE DO WE GO FROM HERE? 99

A FEW FINAL FINANCIAL DO'S & DON'TS 103

HOMEWORK, EXERCISES AND PROJECTS 123

GIVING CREDIT WHERE CREDIT IS DUE 131

APPENDIX A – BALANCE YOUR CHECKBOOK IN FIVE EASY STEPS 137

APPENDIX B – HOW TO READ A BASIC STOCK TICKER 141

APPENDIX C - RECOMMENDED WEB LINKS . 145

APPENDIX D – SMALL BUSINESS START-UP CHECKLIST 147

PREFACE

Why another book on personal finance? Because so many people need guidance in this area. There can never be too many resources outlining current principles on how to gain and maintain control of your finances. This book is intended for people facing challenges in managing their finances, those having difficulty keeping debt to a minimum, those who are unable to save and invest as much as they would like, and especially those who simply want a fresh perspective on today's methods of obtaining and maintaining financial fitness.

Do you worry about money? Do you have a safety net of cash readily available for emergencies? Does your monthly expenses exceed your monthly income? Have you considered how you will fund your retirement so that you can live comfortably? Have you allotted adequate savings or investments for your children's education? Do you want to know how to keep more of what you earn for yourself? Common sense solutions to these and many related questions are addressed in this book.

Compared to other developed countries, the U.S. economy is one of the best; yet so many people are not in control of their finances. In recent years, consumer debt and personal bankruptcy filings have continually increased. Most likely because we are a see it, want it, buy it, and charge it society.

Many of us have not educated ourselves on how to properly manage our finances. In this book, you will learn that sound money management habits and understanding personal finance are not rocket science. You will learn that most people already have the resources to get started increasing their wealth, but simply need a plan, guidance, and proof that achieving wealth is possible.

Hopefully, from this material, you will learn ways to obtain and maintain control of your finances by reducing debt, saving, investing, and enjoying a rewarding life without a barrage of strict and difficult-to-follow limitations on your spending.

Warning – Disclaimer

This book is designed to provide information about aspects of personal finance. It is sold with the understanding that the publisher and author are not engaged in rendering legal, accounting, or other professional services. If legal or expert assistance is required, the services of a competent professional in that field should be acquired.

It is not the purpose of this book to reprint all information that is available to the author or publisher, but to complement and supplement other texts. You should read other material and learn as much as you can on personal finance and wealth building principles. Every effort has been made to make this book as concise and accurate as possible, but there may be mistakes, both typographical and in content. Therefore, this book should be used only *as a guide* and not an ultimate resource on the subject matter. The author and publisher shall have neither liability nor responsibility to any person or entity with respect to any loss or damage caused, or alleged to be caused, directly or indirectly, by the information contained in this book. **If you do not wish to be bound by all of the above, you may return this book to the publisher for a full refund.**

INTRODUCTION

What would it take to make you rich or wealthy? Well, let's look at the *WordWeb Dictionary's* definitions of those adjectives. "**Rich**: Possessing material wealth; Having an abundant supply of desirable qualities or substances (especially natural resources); Of great worth or quality; Marked by great fruitfulness; Strong, intense; Very productive; Marked by richness or fullness of flavor; Pleasantly full and mellow. **Wealthy**: Having an abundant supply of money or possessions of value."

Either rich or wealthy sounds like a good state in which to be, doesn't it? It's what most of us strive for. Living in such a cash conscious and materialistic world, it's only natural to want to possess material things. It's only natural to want to be healthy and enjoy abundance in all aspects of life. How is it that some people have so much, living far above the poverty line, while so many others have so little? Obviously, some are born into wealth, others struggle and achieve it over time, some constantly work towards achieving it, but earn just enough to live comfortably, while others never come close and live from check to check. Why do some people have the discipline to save, invest, and the drive to continually achieve and amass great wealth? Perhaps they are like a lot of us [especially me] in that they had to endure tough lessons early in life that inspired them to educate themselves in the area of personal finance and money management skills, and subsequently made changes based on those lessons and what they learned.

This book is not intended to make anyone independently wealthy overnight. It is not an answer to all financial woes of the world. It is simply a very good common sense guide of suggestions proven to help us reach our financial goals. These suggestions are based on my personal experiences and useful information learned over the years. The author is not a Certified Public Accountant, or Wall Street Analyst, and is not filthy rich as we measure wealth in the world today. I do, however, to the letter, fit the textbook description and definitions of rich and wealthy described above. I want for nothing, do not worry about money, have a few pennies saved and invested, and have planned for a comfortable and hopefully protracted retirement. I am not saying that to be a braggart; I am simply stating facts. I know all too well where I came from, where I am, and have a good idea where I am headed. I didn't become this way overnight and anything I own [material or intangible] certainly did not come easily.

Read on and hopefully you will learn how I came to meet those definitions. You will learn that a little discipline, restraint, and persistence, along with un-learning lifelong self-gratification and unbridled spending habits, will pay off for you in the long run.

Financial literacy and independence, like any other aspects of success, will take diligence, commitment, and work. Yet the end results are well worth the effort.

WHY AND WHERE TO START

Are you interested in quick and easy methods to achieve wealth and financial security? If so, please pass this book on to someone more intelligent, level headed, and realistic because no such method exists. If you are to gain anything from this book, you must understand at the outset that there is no free ride to riches. There is no quick means of achieving lasting wealth (at least no legal means)! To achieve anything worthwhile, it will take a hunger for more than the ordinary, a thirst for a life beyond mediocrity, a burning desire to be above and not beneath.

What does it mean to be *"Above Only and Anxious For Nothing?"* Aside from the biblical connotation, let's talk about the textbook meaning. The dictionary defines **above** as an adverb: "In or to a place that is higher," and the verb **anxious** as an adjective: "Mentally upset over possible misfortune or danger etc; worried." Therefore, to be above only and anxious for nothing in terms of your finances means to be in a higher place in terms of your wealth, your job or business, your home, your attire, and most importantly, your character. It also means not being upset or having to worry about debt; confidently knowing you are able to afford and can obtain and do anything you choose; and being satisfied and content about your financial security today and in the future.

Having explained that, let's talk more about why and where to begin. Start with your attitude. To obtain and keep financial wealth and want for nothing, you have to live a life that promotes prosperity and draws wealth to you. You must believe that you ***deserve*** to enjoy the abundance of wealth available to you. You have to know that you can have virtually ANYTHING you want. Work towards achieving characteristics of a successful, confident, wealthy individual. One such characteristic is integrity. Here are a few ways of maintaining integrity:

1. Always do what you know is morally right and treat people the same way you want to be treated. Respect their rights and opinions. Keep your promises.
2. Celebrate and be thankful for the success and prosperity of others. Avoid jealousy and enviousness.
3. Be genuine, and when problems arise, be first to forgive and do not harbor resentment or hold grudges.
4. Be a good listener, try not to involve yourself in gossip and destructive conversation.

Remember, *when you do the right thing by others, your mind is free of distractions to concentrate on doing what you have to do to reach your goals and enjoy a rich and wealthy life.* Be responsible by educating yourself on the many aspects of the financial world. Share your knowledge at every opportunity. If you are aware of wealth building and money saving tips, share them with your family and friends so that they too can benefit from your experiences.

Look in the mirror at the end of every day and ask yourself whether you have intentionally or unintentionally said or done anything to harm others or yourself. If you decide that you have, do what you can to make it right and promise yourself that you will prevent it from happening again. We are not in this world to suffer, lack, and want for all the abundance of riches and wealth that surrounds us. It is all here for a purpose, and that purpose is for us to enjoy it.

If you are single and looking, understand that no one wants to be bothered with an uninformed, and financially challenged individual. If you expect to nab a formidable and compatible mate, you must bring something to the table. What may help, is an understanding of personal finance and good money management skills. Informed prospective partners need mates who have their own finances in order, not someone seeking a meal ticket, or bringing with them adverse financial baggage in the form of bills and poor money management habits. Being financially responsible will automatically manifest itself in everything you do and potential mates will wear a path to your door. If you are "above only" you will not have to settle for the first thing that comes along, you can afford to and should be selective.

If you are married or in an otherwise committed relationship, one way to keep it alive and vibrant is to become financially fit by empowering yourself with practical information on the many aspects of personal and business finance. Both of you must be financially literate. You will both make better decisions and complement each other by being aware of all the resources and opportunities available to you. By practicing sound financial habits, you will provide a good example for your children.

Whatever your situation, identify **why you** want to make a change in the first place and know that you have the ability to make that change. It is my opinion that many people know what they need to do to become financially fit, but lack the initiative needed to pull it off because they have not defined why they need to make a change. They claim they want financial security, but don't want to do what is necessary to get it. They try principle after principle and technique after technique looking for easy and fast ways to riches and wealth. Let me assure you again, they don't exist. Anything you can conceive, which you genuinely want, you can obtain. You simply have to want it badly enough. You have to have some driving force inside you, either as a negative enforcement, a dream, or positive goal that you're targeting, to put you on the path and keep you there.

Let me give you a few examples of key experiences from my past that drove me to the point of becoming serious about making a change. I know now that back then I had enough money to control my finances, but didn't have the knowledge or discipline to do so. I had to repeatedly endure many setbacks and temporary defeats to push me in the right direction. Everything from bounced checks to having my car repossessed.

- I was introduced to the world of credit in my late teens when I applied for an account at a local jewelry store in Baltimore. No one else would give me credit, being so young and newly employed. But this store gave me a chance by allowing me to open an account. I was very proud of myself. I charged a birthstone ring using a hefty down payment. After I paid them on time for about a year, I applied for a Department Store card and got it. Months later I received a MasterCard in the mail (unsolicited). I was in the big league now. I was on a constant spending spree. Later another card arrived. I started applying for more cards. Pretty soon I had every major credit card and department store card available. It was not long before I was over my head in debt, with accounts charged to their limits. I can recall going to the registers to check out, looking through a handful of cards trying to figure out which one had the most credit available. I eventually pawned the ring, never to reclaim it, yet I still had not paid it off. I was out of control.

- I went to a self-help non-profit agency (highly recommended for those serious about getting out of debt), Consumer Credit Counseling Service (CCCS) who took control of all my bills. All I had to do was send them one affordable payment. They would divide it up among my creditors and mail them payments. They contacted the creditors and arranged to have them accept what they sent. It is a very good agency; however, at the time, I was not serious about getting out of debt. I was simply tired of eluding the hounding creditors and shuffling all the bills. I was not yet tired of my financial situation. The counselors at CCCS came up with a payment plan that was comfortable for me. They advised me that if I missed payments, they would send all the bills back to me. I did; and they did. Back to square one.

- Bill collectors were dunning me at work and at home. I was afraid to answer my own telephone. I had no peace, even in the sanctity of my own home. I was being chased by collection agencies who were looking to make that commission by collecting on my debt. In those days it was not illegal for them to harass you at work. Getting called to the phone by my supervisor who almost always listened in constantly embarrassed me. She offered to send me to employee counseling to get help. I declined. It was demeaning to me, knowing that she was aware of my financial troubles, but still not demeaning enough for me to change. I was so gullible; collectors often tricked me into calling them back by leaving messages with common names like "Call Linda" or "Call Barbara." If it wasn't an 800 number, I usually fell for it thinking it was someone I knew.

- At one point, I was so far behind in my car payment the "Repo" man was looking for my automobile. I had to park my car 6 blocks away from my apartment to prevent them from taking it. The finance company finally caught up with me one night when I returned home too tired to walk the 6 blocks and parked in front of my apartment. I awoke the next morning to the inevitable; my car was gone. I called the police (denial). The first thing they asked was if the payments were current. Ha! Ha! Ha! They had repossessed my car, returned it to the dealer, and parked it in the front row of the dealership. This was totally humiliating and embarrassing. I had to ride the transit bus to work and bum rides, lying to my friends and family that my car was "in the shop." I eventually managed to put together the back payments, late fees, and repossession fees to reclaim my vehicle. Since that day, I have "tried" to make my car payment a priority.

- I was too lazy to read credit card applications, disclosure statements and issuer agreements. There are many tricks and cons they have in store for the consumer. It is amazing they are allowed to get away with them. But they do get away with it because they usually tell you everything in writing. You just have to take the time to READ the fine print. I normally did not. They got me for quite awhile with hidden fees, credit insurance, the gracious privilege of skipping a payment, and free gifts for trying their card. And by now everyone knows about the introductory teaser rate that jumps to exorbitant proportions after a few months (pure usury). I was a sucker for them all.

I recall those "easy to use" convenience checks that I could use to "pay off other higher interest rate bills," or "finance that new car or vacation," according to the inserts and letters they sent. I was too naive (being kind here) to read the portion that spelled out all the added charges and rules for this "privilege." There was usually a 2% or greater fee along with a transaction fee every time I used one of those so called convenience checks. There is a price to pay for ignorance (from not reading the fine print), and I paid heavily.

- Even when I started to earn a good salary, I was still trifling in paying my bills on time. I would often wait until the very last minute to pay the utility companies. One day I started going through mail that had sat around unopened for days, and found a "Second" cut off notice from the electric company. I chuckled, threw it on the table and went on to undress after a tiring day's work. I stepped into the walk-in closet and hit the light switch, no light. I figured hmmm, bulb must have blown. I went to the bedroom wall switch and flipped it on, no light. Maybe a power outage, yet I heard music from the next apartment. Starting to panic now, I ran into other rooms flipping switches to no avail; there was no juice; I began crying like a fool.

I got myself together and called the electric company to arrange for them to reactivate my service (yes, I had the money). They said they couldn't send anyone until the next day. Agony. I sat down on the sofa and had a pity party when I realized it was getting dark. It was normal for my co-workers to drop by after work for cocktails and to play cards. Suddenly realizing this, I got up, closed all the curtains to give the effect of my not being home. The car! What about the car? I thought about moving it, but decided it was too risky. Someone might be pulling up, and it would be impossible to explain. I was too embarrassed to face anyone. Pride is something else. I stayed up most of the night with no lights, no television, no music, and no food. I vowed to never let that happen to me again.

- I ran short on pocket money from check to check. I began to get irritated with little nuisances, such as not being able to fill my tank with gasoline, making multiple trips to the service station buying $5 and $10 worth of gas. I was so busy enjoying life and sowing my wild oats, I neglected to perform the required preventive maintenance on my car. I would buy gas and go, and go, and go, yet expected it to run properly. I was irritated and surprised when problems arose. Duh! These problems were usually expensive to correct; more wasted funds that could have been put to better use.

- My personal checks were beating me home. I knew only too well the embarrassment and shame that comes along with bouncing check after check, paying those exorbitant fees from the "bouncee" and the bank, and the disgrace of having an account closed because of so many rubber checks and insufficient funds. Merchants would sometimes refuse to accept checks after checking on my records prior to sales.

- I used to take pride in remembering family and friends on their birthdays, anniversaries, and holidays. I would go out of my way to buy gifts or give cash or checks. I would run credit cards to the max buying costly gifts. When the bills arrived I would wonder how they got so high and how I was going to pay them and stay on top of everything else.

These experiences drove me to the breaking point. I finally decided to get my finances in order. These powerful memories keep me on the right track, towards achieving my goals today. So many of us have repeatedly experienced the same things or worse, and we have grown accustomed to handling them without learning from them. If you continue to do what you have always done, you will continue to get the same results. So don't adapt to bad situations by handling them and waiting for the next bad situation.

Don't allow yourself to get comfortable finding ways to handle problems without attacking their causes to prevent them from occurring in the future.

I set two goals: 1) To build a savings account with a *specific* amount of emergency money, and 2) To pay off credit card debt. This was only after experiencing sheer frustration, getting sick and tired of going without, and getting tired of allowing myself to be a victim. It was not easy, but somehow I managed to do it, over time, with the help of God. If I can do it, you can too!

Try not to repeat the same mistakes, learn from them. Most importantly, avoid beating yourself up because you have repeated the same mistakes. Look at financial failures as stepping stones, lessons, and significant events that had to take place to mold you into the financially fit wealthy individual that you want to be.

Take responsibility for *your* past mistakes. You should take a few moments to list some of *your own* embarrassing blunders, hard lessons, financial hardships and past errors that were particularly humiliating. It does not have to be detailed or descriptive, just include enough information to trigger the memory of the experience. This "lessons learned" list of experiences may be useful later when you are tempted to sway from your goals toward financial fitness. Now let's talk about goals.

ESTABLISH YOUR GOALS

Before you can obtain anything, you have to know exactly what you want. To say you want to be financially fit is too broad. You have to have some specific goal(s) to work towards: goals you want so badly and desperately, that the very thought of them is powerful enough to keep you on track when your human weakness attempts to derail you from your path towards financial fitness and freedom.

Take time out to think about exactly what you want to accomplish with added income and decreased expenses. Think about what drives you. Are you more apt to stay on track by remembering the powerful experiences that branded themselves into your very being? Are you driven by the desire for something specific? Or are you driven by both positive and negative reinforcement? I hope you want to make that change badly enough. I hope you are literally sick of not being able to achieve what you want in the area of finances. I hope you are angry enough about not having enough to do what it takes to get and keep more of what you deserve. In order to get and stay on the right path towards financial independence, you must be obsessed with the idea of building wealth and determined not to let anything or anyone deter you from your goals.

Start by establishing a target and developing specific goal(s) in the financial arena. List at least three realistic things you would do with increased income and decreased or no bad debt. Bad debt is credit card debt, personal signature loans, and any debt that is not tax deductible or that does not appreciate or otherwise maintain value in the long term. Examples of good debt are a home mortgage, business or educational loan.

Here are a few thought provoking questions to help you start thinking about short, mid, and long term goals:

1. What tangible material possessions do you want most?
2. What realistic amount in your investment portfolio would make you feel totally relaxed and financially secure?
3. Who are the most important people in your life, and what would you like to accomplish on their behalf?
4. Where do you want to live when you retire and what will you do?
5. Where do you see yourself financially in 5 years, 10 years, 20 years?
6. If there was one fun thing you could do every day of your life, what would that be?
7. What single accomplishment do you want to achieve in a year?

Establish a vision of where you see yourself financially in the future, then think about the steps required to realize that vision. Some examples of realistic financial goals could be to pay off all credit card debt (list each card and the balance); to save a down payment on a house (specify how much of a down payment and include settlement costs and moving expenses); to pay off an existing mortgage; to finance an education for you or your children; to establish an emergency fund (most experts advise 2-6 months of expenses); to invest and save for retirement; to retire early; to purchase a new wardrobe; to establish or build your investment portfolio; to buy a vacation home; or to start your own business. Be specific; for example, don't say, "remodel the house." Break it down to what room or item you want to remodel or replace first. Whichever goals you choose, make sure you are ready to receive them, to take responsibility and do what it takes to get them, and to give up whatever is necessary to make room for them.

Prioritize these things. **WRITE THEM DOWN**. The first (short term goals) should be attainable within 3-6 months; the second (mid-term goals) should be attainable within 6 months to a year; and the third (long-term goals) should be attainable from 1 to 3 years or more. How soon you reach the goals will depend on your current financial condition, your level of discipline and self-control, and the degree of determination and dedication you apply towards reaching them.

Under each goal, list the steps you need to take to reach the goal. Apply target dates to each of the goals and their subordinate steps. Put the list of your top three goals (without the specific steps needed to reach them) in plain view where you will see it daily. Preferably somewhere private and inaccessible to those outside of your immediate family (dresser mirror, closet, sun visor in your car, inside flap of your portfolio or briefcase, your wallet or purse, etc.). You should not reveal it to anyone other than your spouse or trusted partner. If you must post your list where others can see it, use code words to describe the goals that only you recognize.

Couples will have an edge by developing the goals list together, establishing mutual goals or some goals for each of you and some you both agree upon. Later on you can encourage and help each other stay on the path towards the goals.

Concentrate on those goals at every opportunity. Speak and affirm them to your inner self, and out loud whenever possible. Imagine yourself with whatever it is you have set as your goal, think of it as often as you see the list. Feel it, smell it, taste it, anticipate and experience it. Plan what you will do once you have it; picture this in detail in your mind's eye. Believe that you truly deserve what you are working towards. Know that God intended for you to be successful and prosperous and wants you to have whatever it is you want.

Whenever you feel you are losing focus and tend to sway away from your goal, concentrate on the goals to bring you back. For example, if you are working towards buying a new home, drive through the neighborhood you are targeting, have a real estate agent show you properties similar to those you are aiming for, or draw up a draft of the plans for the interior of the house. If it is an automobile you're working towards, test drive one with all the accessories you will buy. If starting a business is your target, visit a similar company, then research and learn as much as possible about the daily operation of the specific type of business.

Try reviewing and reliving the experiences on your "lessons learned" list. Perhaps that may remind you of where you never want to be again. If focusing on the goal or reflecting on why you established the goal does not work, you have chosen the wrong goal. It must be something that YOU desperately want, not what someone else has chosen for you.

Once you start to accomplish the goals, periodically review the list and always replace an accomplished goal with a new one. Keep your list current and based on your financial situation, lifestyle, and mind set. Set a date to update the entire goals list. I use two holidays to step back, reflect, regroup, and plan my next moves. July 4th and January 1st are two good milestones for reflecting and planning.

I realize some people are not fond of lists. However, it is very important to list your goals, because lists enable you to focus on them and prioritize them. Writing them down keeps them in the forefront of your mind, and you are less apt to forget them. You should feel proud when you are able to cross goals off the list as you accomplish them.

Remember also that it is extremely important to reward yourself for your successes. As you pay off a debt, or otherwise accomplish steps in your list of goals, don't hesitate to treat yourself to something you enjoy as a reward.

SAMPLE Goals List (part of your financial plan)

1. Pay off credit card debt in 2 years
2. Increase retirement savings immediately

Breakdown of specific steps needed to reach each goal listed:

1. Pay off credit card debt (ABC Bank by XX/XX).

ACTION	DATE
Cut up ABC Bank credit card with $3100 outstanding balance.	XX/XX
Optional: Withdraw $1500 from savings, apply it to balance on ABC Bank card.	XX/XX
Send double minimum payment monthly on remaining balance. Triple if possible.	XX/XX - XX/XX
Receive 0 balance statement from ABC Bank.	XX/XX
Prepare and mail letter to bank requesting account to be closed. Celebrate.	XX/XX
Repeat above steps with next credit card or loan, update dates accordingly.	XX/XX

2. Increase retirement savings immediately.

ACTION	DATE
Contact personnel department, financial advisor, or bank to discuss options available.	XX/XX
Either through payroll deductions or automatic withdrawals from checking increase contributions to existing retirement account or begin initial deposits.	XX/XX
Optional: If 10 years or less to retirement, enroll in a pre-retirement seminar or class.	XX\XX
Optional: If possible, in one year, increase amount being contributed.	XX/XX - XX/XX

NOTE: This list contains *sample* data only. It is being provided to depict the necessity to list your goals, with specific steps required to reach the goal, and due dates for each step. Replace XX/XX with the target date.

TRACK YOUR EXPENSES

Once you understand why you need to make a change in managing your finances, and you focus on realistic goals you strongly desire, you can now begin to take additional steps toward achieving those goals. You must first learn to wisely use what you already have before you look to obtain more.

First and foremost, you have to assess your current situation. You have to know where you are to determine which path to take towards getting where you want to be. Common sense, right? When traveling in an unfamiliar town most people purchase a map. In order to find out how to get to a certain point, you must first find where you are on the map, identify your destination, plot the best course towards your destination by listing the different turns and roads to take, then head there. This common sense approach is basic to most things in life, especially when working toward financial fitness.

Start by tracking your expenses for a week, then for a month. You should do this for **AT LEAST SIX MONTHS** to get a realistic idea of all expenditures. Record everything you buy or pay money toward. Carry a small pad and document every dime you spend. I know it's going to take a little effort, and might seem cheap or tedious at first, but the end result will surprise and even shock you.

If you don't have the self control and discipline to track expenditures monthly, try it for a week, then increase it to two weeks, then three until you can account for at least two to six months of expenses. Once you get a handle on where your income is going, you can focus in on areas where you can reduce spending or redirect wasted dollars towards something more productive and likely to pay off in the longer term.

There are literally hundreds of books and thousands of resources on the Internet to help you track expenses. Once you have listed your expenses, you will need to group them into categories. Start with three simple categories. Try to list at least ten items in each category. Here is a quick method of categorizing what you have tracked that worked for me, one that best suited my circumstances:

Category A for required, fixed, and unavoidable expenses that we all have (basic needs);
Category B for desirable items, but things which are not true necessities, things you could do without if times were rough and challenging; and
Category C for things that if you had to go without, would not decrease your quality of life or send you to the corner with a tin cup.

Here's a typical list, create your own and record how much you pay out to each one based on your records tracking your spending:

A: Mortgage, rent, charitable donation, grocery, transportation, child care, utilities (Gas, electric, phone, & water), savings, investments, insurance, vacation, prescription drugs, medical visits, taxes, etc.

B: Credit card, cell phone, internet access, lunch at the local steak house, lawn or maid service, pager, new attire, pedicure, gifts, allowance, health club membership, barber/hairdresser, pet grooming, etc.

C: Dinner & show, movie theatre, season tickets to the ball games, bingo, cigarettes, lottery subscription, dance lessons, alcohol (beer, wine, liquor), summer camp, magazine subscriptions, cable TV, video rental, music CD purchase, snacks at work, etc.

The intent is for you to record all expenditures, no matter how small, and categorize them. Use whatever format is comfortable for you, but don't make it complicated; keep it simple. Listing expenditures in detail can be a sobering and sometimes frightening experience. It was for me. Don't let it panic or discourage you, but use the experience as a wake-up call to make a change. Use your checkbook if necessary to help determine where money is spent. On the next page is an alternate example of what your chart might look like:

MONTHLY EXPENSES

Mortgage/Rent: _____
Transportation: _____
Utilities: _____
Savings/Investments: _____
Taxes: _____
Insurance: _____
Grocery: _____
Clothing: _____
Medical: _____
Child care: _____
Entertainment: _____
Magazine Subscriptions: _____
Credit Card: _____
Credit Card: _____
Charity: _____
Other: _____
Other: _____

TOTAL
MONTHLY EXPENSES: _____

For best results you will want to break these categories down to specifically show where your funds are spent.

Now record all sources of your monthly income. Include any income received on a regular basis [not overtime] such as salaries & wages, alimony payments, interest, dividends, etc.

Try this simple test to decide whether you need to make adjustments. Total your monthly expenses, then total your monthly income. Subtract your expenses from your income.

Total Monthly Income: _____

Total Monthly Expenses: _____

Difference: _____

If your income exceeds your expenses, you are one of the fortunate ones. The amount of money you have left over can be used to help you reach your goals. If the difference is minimal, you may still need to make some changes to free up additional cash to help you reach your goals. **_Reality Check_**: Experts say your total monthly expenses, excluding your mortgage should be no more than 20 percent of your net income.

If your expenses surpass your income, don't worry. You have a little work to do in terms of making adjustments to generate more cash to help you attain your goals. I prefer to do this without the "B" word (budget). You can now use some of the guidelines and steps outlined in the remainder of this book to develop a plan of action towards your financial well being.

Remember the three categories you created earlier? Determine where the lion's share of your spending goes in each category. Create sub-categories under each one if you need to, but keep them under the basic three.

You can now select five things from Category "C" and get rid of them, cancel them. Cease and desist financing them immediately. If you are not a strong-willed person, do this with three instead, and work your way to alleviating five. If you are very strong and really want to better yourself sooner than later, stop all Category "C" items, at least temporarily (1 or 2 years) until you can truly afford them (when you are free of bad debt and in control of your finances).

If you used the alternative method of listing your expenditures, just look for areas that are non-essential where you could cut back or otherwise redirect those funds into something more productive.

CUT EXPENSES AND INCREASE INCOME

You now have a general idea of where you are financially in terms of income and expenses. And, you have identified three or more specific, yet realistic goals you want to reach. You have identified where most of your money goes outside of your fixed expenses. You have stopped purchasing some of the non-critical items, and if you are bold, cut back or discontinued a few of the Category B items.

All of this should free up cash you can use to apply to outstanding bills, if you have any. If debt is already under control, use the cash you have freed up to start or increase savings and investments; more on this later. The next steps involve taking more action towards increasing your income to free up even more cash needed to move you closer to those goals.

Let's start with a few *proven* solutions towards personal wealth building by putting more money in your pocket immediately. These should not decrease your quality of life or cost you anything other than the little time it takes to invoke them. They are quick short-term solutions, but pay off big time in the long haul.

Simple steps to IMMEDIATELY increase your income and decrease your monthly expenses

1. Start your own business. It is not as complicated as you may think. See Appendix D for a check list of things you need to consider. You can establish a business in your community, or begin with a home-based business. Either way you can set up a sole proprietorship, partnership, or corporation. There are many free resources on the Internet and at your local library on everything from how to develop a business plan to where to find start up capital. Find your niche, something you enjoy and excel at, and use it to your financial advantage. Some examples that can bring in extra cash from home are tutoring, child care, lawn service, chauffeuring and running errands for the elderly, painting, creating gift baskets, selling cosmetics or household items and staples, business consulting services, tax preparation, financial planning, house sitting services, employment and recruitment services, etc.

If you have a home computer your choices are limitless. For example, companies are always looking for people to do data entry, contract and freelance programmers, transcribers, and typeset input operators. Try searching on any of those key words using your favorite search engine on the Internet.

If you are willing to use your automobile in a home based business, there are many mobile services that cater to the busy population, such as auto detailing, washing and polishing, catering, pet grooming, oil changing service, windshield repair and scratch removal, etc.

Other businesses that have a good track record and show promise include insurance or real estate sales, legal services, any kind of gift shop, restaurant, or anything directly or indirectly related to the health care industry.

2. Increase your withholding allowances to prevent getting a big tax refund. Why should you give the Government all that money to hold and invest during the year only to get a fat refund with no interest? You can put that money to good use yourself. Talk to your payroll office or tax consultant first to make sure you don't overdo it; they have ways of approximating your tax liability to ensure the right amount is withheld. The last thing you need is to owe Uncle Sam.

3. Cancel those fun-to-have but unnecessary features on your telephone. Do you really need to know who's calling before you answer the telephone? Unless you have a business, do you have to be able to conference and talk to more than one person at a time?

Think about the special ring feature, where you can specify a ring sequence for certain members of the household? Have we gotten so lazy now we don't even want to pick up the phone unless we know it's for us? Apparently some of us with teenagers have gotten that lazy. Instead of paying that astronomical telephone bill, invest a few dollars in a decent answering machine and cancel that phone company voice mail account. Add up the cost of the voice mail over just 6 months and you have paid for the best feature-packed answering machine on the market.

There are so many other services that we could live without if only we were serious about getting out of debt and building wealth. Call forward, call block, call this, call that! If you absolutely have to have some features, see if the telephone company has single-use pricing on the same service. We have to start somewhere; so why not start by eliminating optional features and added services of convenience? You can surely get as many as you want, once you are in control of your finances.

4. Ask for a raise. If you are employed, and are doing your absolute best in contributing to the success of your company, there is nothing wrong with speaking up for yourself. Throughout your employment, you should be involved in projects that make you stand out among others. Step up and volunteer for

assignments that most people would shun. Don't watch the clock; stay until the job is done. Submit suggestions and constructive criticism on ways to improve the business. Keep yourself marketable by taking classes related to your field. Make yourself an asset to the company so that your management automatically recognizes you. When you go in to ask for the raise, there should be little or no negotiation if you have set the stage by contributing above and beyond what was expected.

5. Cancel premium channel(s) on cable or satellite. You can do this temporarily if you are looking for a quick way to reduce the amount you have to pay for things you don't really need, and that will not reduce your quality of life if you let them go. You can do them permanently if you have the discipline to go without frills and extra features. For example, most cable companies offer several packages of premium channels that you hardly ever watch. How many channels can you watch at the same time anyway? If you carry three premium channels, reduce it to two. If you carry two, reduce it to one favorite channel.

If you can restructure your life to do something other than be a couch potato, cancel the cable account altogether for 1 or 2 years until you feel you are in better control of your finances. If you are serious about building wealth, surely you can endure at least temporarily, broadcast TV and their commercials as you did before there was cable. You may find you don't even miss the cable or satellite service.

Paying for this service is really cost prohibitive if you rent Digital Video Disks (DVD's) or video tapes, because some of the same rentals you have paid for will eventually show up on cable and satellite. If you are a "movie-aholic" check out your local library, since many now rent DVD's and video tapes for much less and some can be borrowed at no charge. Read a book, surf the Internet, find constructive but fun alternatives to television.

6. Increase your insurance deductibles to decrease the premiums. If you carry a higher deductible, say $250 or even $500 instead of the traditional $50 or $100, you can decrease your insurance premium substantially. This is almost like insuring yourself and pays off big time in the long run. Try this for Auto, Renter's, or Homeowner's insurance.

Be careful with this one, especially auto insurance, because bad things happen to good people. Make sure you are willing and able to pay the higher deductible if you have an accident. Slow down, drive safely and perhaps you will even qualify for a safe driver rate.

Remember, auto insurance rates are based on several factors such as:

- Your driving habits as reflected on your driving record,
- How you use your car, whether it is for work, pleasure or both, and the number of miles you drive,
- The kind of cars you own. More expensive vehicles will cost more to repair and replace, therefore premiums will be higher,
- Your age and sex, because younger male drivers tend to be less cautious than more mature drivers,
- Where you live, because the number of accidents and claims varies and tend to be higher in larger busy metropolitan areas,
- and others.

7. Decide whether you really need to carry full coverage (comprehensive and collision) on older vehicles. If the vehicle is substantially old you may want to drop the extra coverage. An accident that results in major damage or even totals an older car can put you in the red, because you can only recoup insurance for the value of the car.

8. Compare insurance rates, do the math, and change companies if it makes sense. At least once every 2 years you should do this. Set aside a day and take the

time to pick up the phone book and contact various insurance agencies and get quotes on the same amounts of coverage. There are websites that help you do this quite painlessly (see Appendix C). Have your existing policies nearby.

If you are contemplating buying another vehicle you may want to call your insurance company first to see what the premium will be. Try to find companies that deal directly with you. Perhaps cutting out the middleman may also save. You can factor this into your decision as to which vehicle to purchase. When I was in the market for a 4X4 sport utility vehicle, I was told my policy would be cancelled if I bought a certain make of 4X4. They gave me estimated premiums for the ones in which I expressed interest.

9. Talk to your insurer about discounts. Some insurance companies will give you a good discount in premiums if you have certain safety features in your home or car (alarm system, fire extinguisher, dead bolt locks, or smoke detectors). Ask about them. Some companies will cut your premiums if you have your auto, health, and homeowner's or renter's insurance policies with them. Dealing with one company can be convenient for you, but do your research to get the best coverage for your dollar.

Some companies will reduce your premium if you agree to pay annually or quarterly instead of monthly. This applies to several types of insurance. This reduces their expenses, which they sometimes pass on to you.

10. Negotiate a lower interest rate on your credit card(s). People are getting smarter by not running up credit cards to their limit, and by paying them off and destroying the cards. This has resulted in the credit card companies desperately competing for your business. If you have a high interest rate card that you know you cannot pay off within 1-6 months, call the company and tell them you're considering transferring the balance to a lower interest rate card but would prefer to stay with their firm if they could offer a lower rate. They will probably match or offer you a lower rate. If you have more than one credit card, destroy all but one major card, and make sure you keep the one with the lowest interest rate and no annual fee. Cut them up into unusable strips. As you pay them off, you will write the company and direct them to close those accounts.

11. Work overtime if it is available to you. Even if it is not a common practice at your company, some managers and business owners may be willing to spring for it (time and a half) if it will pay off for the company. So ask your boss if overtime is available.

12. Sell something that is no longer of use to you, but in good condition and may be useful to others. For example, that expensive exercise equipment you may have bought but didn't quite get a chance to use, or that Vitavetavegimin-like appliance you bought off the infomercial that didn't pan out to be as nifty as you thought. See what other dust collectors you have around that you can turn into cash. You can sell them on ebay, via your local paper, yard sale or flea market.

13. Look into the feasibility of converting whole life insurance policies into much less expensive term insurance. Although this can save you a bundle, be careful because term insurance is not always practical for every situation. Do your research, especially if you have others that rely on your income. Be cautious with buying mortgage insurance which can be very expensive, whereas term insurance can usually be obtained more economically and in greater amounts.

14. Cancel magazine subscriptions. If this is difficult for you and you feel you absolutely MUST have them, keep one favorite that really enriches you in some way, one you will read regularly. Let the others go. Examples include canceling the television or cable guides if you buy the daily paper, since most newspapers include television listings. Most cable providers have online listings.

Many local libraries carry all popular magazines for your borrowing pleasure at no charge. A trip to the library can be rewarding, you may bump into a good book or tackle a tape, both of which are more interesting than some of the magazines we buy.

15. Ask for gifts of cash. When people ask me what I want for my birthday, holidays, or other special occasions, I will almost always say CASH. That's right. Be smart. Cash is something we can always use, and you don't have to worry about folks buying you something that will end up in the "stupid gift" drawer. People have given me such idiotic things (that cost good money), which they thought I would like. I end up re-cycling them to someone else or throwing them away. I would have preferred a few dirty dollars tucked into a thoughtful card.

16. Take a local less expensive vacation this year. Vacations are a must, but they don't have to put you further in debt. Investigate local attractions and things to do that don't require the added expense of travel and accommodations. If you do travel, try to make reservations well in advance and be willing to travel at any time of the day or night to get the best rate.

17. Obtain a low interest or no interest loan from a close relative or trusted friend and use those proceeds to pay off a high interest credit card or high interest loan.

Make sure you document the loan agreement in writing and by all means pay them back on time.

18. Compare interest rates on your savings, checking, or money market accounts. Shop around for a better interest rate. If another bank or credit union will pay more without a barrage of fees that could counteract the interest earned, consider switching.

DRASTIC TIMES CALL FOR DRASTIC MEASURES

If you can accomplish most of the previous suggestions, you should be well on your way to financial fitness with increased income. If you want to take it a step further, here are other things you can try temporarily to boost income even higher. ***Reality Check:*** As you take on any of these tasks, keep focused on your goals. If you find yourself getting too far behind the timeframes you have established, don't panic. You simply need to organize anew and make adjustments to your plan.

Some of the following tips may require more sacrifice than you are used to, or are willing to make, but the end result is worth it. What could be worth all this you ask? How about peace of mind in being out of bad debt, having the funds to do more of what YOU want to do, such as moving into that new home, unlocking the door to your own business, depositing your first commission check, pulling off in that new car, walking up to that podium to get that degree, or obtaining whatever other goals you have set. See how many of these drastic measures you can use:

1. Get a part time job. This is the quickest way to accrue more income temporarily or permanently. For example, I sold real estate for a few years. Not only

was it very financially rewarding, but the required training for licensing served to educate me on many facets of banking and finance. I was able to build a network of friends [resources] in several fields, such as bankers and private lenders, notaries, insurance professionals, home inspectors, attorneys, etc. I was able to legally deduct nearly all of the expenses and saved substantially on taxes.

2. Try budget billing, if your utility company offers it. You can arrange to pay a fixed amount every month and reconcile with them annually. This eliminates the surprise whopping heating bills in winter and gigantic air conditioning bills in summer. Consider replacing ancient appliances that waste electricity for more cost efficient energy saving appliances. You can make simple changes around your house that can save you money. For example, repair dripping faucets, install energy saving or washer-less faucets or shower heads that use less water, install insulation around your hot water tank, etc.

3. Avoid giving expensive gifts, or any gifts, to family and friends for a year (or more). Instead, you could donate your time to others, be creative and make personal gifts, or just stick to a thoughtful card.

4. Plan and combine trips to save gas and mileage on your car. If you have to temporarily rent a vehicle, make sure you don't pay for insurance coverage you may already have on your existing auto policy.

5. If you are in the market for a car, consider buying a good used one. Used cars can be better deals in the long run, but have your mechanic thoroughly check it before buying. There are also websites which provide vehicle history (repair, recall, accident, etc.) for a fee. Try www.carfax.com or www.autocheck.com.

6. Buy in bulk to save money. Almost everything is less expensive when bought in large quantities. Shop at membership warehouses if you have freezer and storage space for bulk purchases. For a large family, a freezer is a good investment and should save money.

7. Quit smoking. As of this writing cigarettes cost about $800 a year for a "pack a day" smoker. Besides the financial savings, you will most likely live longer, enjoy your food more, kiss sweeter, and feel better overall.

8. If you purchase prescription drugs, ask your doctor or pharmacist whether you can take generic equivalents. This can save you hundreds of dollars a year. Check the Internet for reputable companies that handle mail order prescriptions. This can also save you a bundle.

9. Consider carrying the legal minimums of coverage on your auto insurance. This will save you loads of money, but is risky in today's litigious society, so be extremely cautious with this one. Your personal assets may be at risk if you are sued [and lose] for an amount more than your insurance will cover.

10. Carpool or use public transportation. Do the math, and if it is more economical to double up or ride the subway for a while, why not?

11. Move into a smaller, less expensive dwelling. This is quite drastic, but can save you a lot of money. If this idea makes you cringe, consider temporarily taking in a boarder to offset the cost of rent or mortgage. Do your research before you allow anyone into your home to live, and lay down all the rules in writing.

12. Refinance your home or car and consolidate that credit card debt if the interest rate AND monthly payments are substantially lower. A lower rate of at least 2 percentage points or more is usually a good rule of thumb for a mortgage refinance. Again, do your homework; research the settlement costs, fees, and life of the loan. Make sure it does not take you deeper into debt. For example: If you are out of control and have not learned to curtail your spending, when you get that lower payment and extra cash (which often accompanies a refinance) you risk

running those credit card bills right back up. You could end up with the original consolidated debt AND the newly charged debt and nowhere to go but south.

13. Make one less trip to the shopping mall this month. Shopping at malls generally costs more anyway. Someone has to pay for those expensive rents the individual storeowners pay and for those beautiful glossy advertisements we receive in the mail. Wear that dress or suit one more time before you "treat" yourself to a new one. Instead of buying a new pair of shoes, if the upper portions are in good condition, have them resoled for a fraction of the price of a new pair and wear them another month or more.

14. Peruse the local paper and magazines for coupons on products you frequently use. Normally I don't make recommendations of things I have not done or are not willing to do. To be honest, I hate using coupons, and mailing in rebates, but both can result in substantial savings.

15. If a spouse is unemployed, but able to work, put him/her to work part-time or full-time until the financial situation is comfortably manageable by one.

16. Look into the possibility of obtaining a low interest loan from your retirement savings. Many accounts

allow you to "borrow from yourself," at substantially lower rates than traditional loans from banks.

These are only *suggestions* for increasing income so that you will have more available cash to help you meet your goals. Perhaps you can come up with more ideas, based on your individual situation. You, and only you, must ultimately decide where and how to reduce spending. You are the one who has to deal with whatever surfaces in the areas you focus on making sacrifices; and you are the one who will reap the benefits.

<u>Reality check</u>: Remember your goals and what's driving you towards them. But more importantly, remember the ultimate goal in attaining financial victory is to **maintain balance** in your life. All sacrifice and hard work without reward, may discourage or deter you from what you are trying to accomplish. Spend some of the funds on yourself and your family. You **must** continue to engage in recreation and entertainment, yet exercise enough discipline to keep your bills paid, tuck something away for emergencies, and invest in your future.

WHAT TO DO WITH THE INCREASED INCOME

You should use your additional income to accomplish the following: 1) reduce debt, 2) save, and 3) invest. Ok, ok, if you must, take a few bucks and reward yourself for your success in freeing up cash, but don't overdo it. Now let's spend that extra cash constructively:

REDUCE DEBT: Debt can be characterized as the new form of slavery, which knows no race or religion. Debt is a cancer eating at our pocketbooks; it is like a 100-foot tall, barbed wire topped brick wall to financial security. We need to do everything possible to reduce and eliminate it. Concentrate on paying off bad credit card debt. This must be your first focus; pay it off. Credit card companies are robbing you without a gun, through high interest, late fees, annual fees, cash advance fees, etc. Consider using a portion of your savings to pay off a high interest credit card or loan debt. It may sound crazy, but if you do the math, you will easily see that thousands of dollars of interest can be 'saved' by paying off the debt. The amount of interest you avoid paying, more than exceeds what you could have earned from the savings account. For example, look at the big picture. Take one of your credit card bills, and calculate how much interest you would pay the company on the existing balance in a year, without even charging anything additional on the card. Now take that amount of interest and compare it to what you would have earned had you not paid off the bill and left the same amount of cash in your savings. Well hello. To make it even simpler, just look at the amount of interest that is added to your credit card balances monthly...can you earn that much interest on cash you have accumulated in a savings account? It should be easier to rebuild your savings once your debt is minimized.

Reality check: This debt reduction method of using partial savings to pay off credit card debt is not practical for everyone, because we all need some level of comfort by maintaining savings for emergencies. Use your good judgment and common sense.

Always pay more than the minimum payment, go with at least double the minimum payment if at all possible. If you can, pay the full balance every month. Just look at this example of how much longer and how much more you would pay if you only paid the minimum payment:

For a loan balance of $5000, at 12% interest:

Monthly Payment	$200	$50 (minimum payment)
Timeframe	3 years	8 years
Total Interest Paid	$800.	$2800.
Total Amount Paid	**$5800.**	**$7800.**

If you receive unexpected gifts of cash or checks, apply some of them to your credit card bills, if you are trying to reduce debt. Attack the ones with the highest interest rate first or ones with the smallest balance first. As you pay off one, apply its payment to the next one. Watch your spending; take care not to run up the balances again, and cut up all but one card.

When you pay off other major bills such as a car or boat, use that payment towards another bill. Until your debt is under control, resist the urge to trade up to the latest model, thereby creating another monthly obligation.

Remember the quicker you are out of debt, the sooner you will have peace of mind and become more capable of affording more for you and your family.

Once you start paying off bills and receiving those zero balance statements, you will experience a very strong sense of accomplishment. Hopefully, it will become addictive and you should be driven to work harder to get the next one paid off. Remember it took time to get into debt and will take time to get out of it. So be realistic and don't get discouraged if it doesn't happen overnight. Keep your eye on what you are trying to accomplish: the security and peace of mind that comes with being debt-free and in control of your finances.

SAVE: Squirrel something away; start small. If you don't have one, open a savings account, preferably a money market or other liquid account (that you can readily access, if necessary). As your income increases deposit something into this account REGULARLY. An automatic payroll deduction into some form of savings is your best bet. This allows you to pay yourself first.

No matter how small, you must put something away and *leave it there.* Your savings record can serve as a powerful tool in terms of proof of your diligence, dedication, and discipline when you need to apply for major loans, such as a car, boat, education, or home loan. The experts advise that we should save 10% of our gross income. If you are unable to do this at first, try to put at least 5% away.

You must act as if the savings account does not exist. Yes, you will be tempted to skip a deposit or withdraw portions of what you have saved. Resist with all your might. Temptation MUST come. It is one of the means that will strengthen you. Stay the course by focusing on your goals and why you are saving. Do not let family and friends know what you have. Some people may have a tendency to borrow indefinitely, or otherwise take advantage of your generosity. If they don't know what you have, they won't continuously develop reasons to borrow or mooch.

If you already have a savings account, or are saving regularly, increase the amount you're saving, if possible. The savings account can be held for a specific goal such as a vacation, or can be maintained as an emergency fund for unexpected expenses. You should shop around for the best interest rates available. If you know that you have a very difficult time leaving your savings alone, put your money into savings vehicles that you cannot get to so easily, such as U.S. savings bonds or certificates of deposit.

INVEST: It is highly unlikely that you will become financially independent on earned income and savings alone, even if you have little or no debt. A wealth builder's financial plan is pretty much doomed to mundane success or even failure, without some phase or steps that include investing. To obtain higher gains, you will have to take higher risks by investing. What is investing? It is simply the act of setting aside money or capital in an enterprise (business), *usually over time*, with the expectation of gaining a profit. For example, you can invest in stocks, bonds, mutual funds, or real estate, to mention a few options.

Over the last few decades stocks have fluctuated, but have consistently outperformed most other investment vehicles. Be careful with this one, as investing will require detailed research as well as professional advice from a financial consultant or a broker who is licensed in securities. Use extreme care when selecting a professional to guide your investing. They should be accredited and participate in continuing education, so their knowledge base is current. Check their track record. There are all sorts of resources at local libraries and on the Internet that specify what to look for in these professionals.

Beware of hot stock tips from your cousin or the neighbor across the fence. Don't heed the advice of every clown that comes along claiming to have unique information on any investment without researching it yourself. Learn the basics of investing so that you will know what to ask and what to look for in a professional. You do not need large sums of money to invest. You only need good common sense, persistence and a little patience. In my opinion, investing is for long term goals such as buying a home, paying for an education, expanding your business, or funding and supplementing retirement.

There is no one size fits all investment strategy. When, how, and where you invest your dollars will depend on a number of things such as your investment goals, your priorities, age, available funds, etc. The key is to do it NOW. If you haven't already, it is never too late to start, the sooner you begin, the better off you will be.

Reality Check: A word to the wise…increased income (more money) is not always the key to getting control of your finances. Controlling your finances simply requires learning to discipline yourself to *live within your means* without sacrificing your quality of life. It requires learning to more effectively manage what you already have by knowing where your money is going, keeping debt to a minimum, and planning for the future by saving for emergencies and investing for the long term.

SEVEN SECRETS "THEY" DON'T WANT YOU TO KNOW

Give, Take, Watch, Optimize, Organize, Maximize, and Party Hearty.

Secret #1: Give. Contribute to charity. From the King James Version of the <u>Bible,</u> Galatians 6:7 reads "Be not deceived, God is not mocked. For whatsoever a man soweth, that shall he also reap." This simply means that whatever you put out there (sow), you will get back (reap). Luke 6:38 reads "Give, and it shall be given unto you; good measure, pressed down, and shaken together, and running over, shall men give into your bosom. For with the same measure that ye mete withal it shall be measured to you again." Of all the Scriptures in the Bible, I have found these to be the most powerful and effective, especially in the area of obtaining financial security and wealth. Actually, they work in all aspects of life where the concept of sowing and reaping would apply. But they work best with finances, because of the inevitable return that results. Whether you believe in biblical principles or not, believe me this works.

All you have to do is faithfully contribute to a charity, your local church, or other preferably non-profit organization, whose focus is to give back to your community. The amount is up to you; but a practical guideline is to strive for 10% of your gross income, the same amount you should be putting away for yourself. If you can give more, all the better.

If it is hard for you to part with cash, consider donating shares of stock to a qualified church or charity. You may get a double benefit if the stock has appreciated since you bought it, because you may be able to avoid the capital gains tax. The contribution can also be in the form of donating food to a soup kitchen, giving useful clothing and household articles in good condition to charitable organizations, sending a check to non-profit research organizations, a volunteer fire department, a national or worldwide ministry, or even to the campaign of a reputable public servant.

Don't worry so much about whom you give to and whether or not they are going to put the gift to proper use. Just use good common sense when selecting a target organization for your gift. A good rule of thumb is to give to organizations which are spiritually benefiting and or inspiring to you, your family, or community. Support charities and organizations that take on tasks that you believe are worthwhile. Know that once you make the contribution, responsibility is also placed on the recipient to put it to good use. You have met your responsibility by giving the gift; they must meet theirs by utilizing it wisely.

All concepts outlined in this book are effective, but this particular [secret] can sure up your plan for certain. Not only will it make you feel even better about yourself, but it also provides for those less fortunate, shares the wealth, and causes a boomerang effect that will propel ***return*** back to you. Strive towards giving the 10%, and do this regularly if you want to maintain a regular return. The proportions of return are always greater than the original seed, so be generous. ***Reality check***: Like everything else, keep this in perspective; by all means don't be stupid by giving away your mortgage, utility, grocery or rent money. Use your own good judgment as to how much, how often, and to whom you contribute.

Remember this is not new, just simple common sense that we often forget about because we sometimes get caught up in our own greed and try to hold onto every dollar. The religious folks may say, "You will reap what you sow." The secular folks might say, "What goes around comes around." The scientific groups say, "For every action there is an opposite or equal reaction." But however it is stated, the concept and end result is the same, and it truly works.

If you have been selfish and tend to think of the "you" instead of the "we" this [secret] may be a little challenging to grasp. But you must grasp it. Try it and you may learn to step outside of yourself. This is key to maintaining wealth, to keeping it continuously flowing in your life. Once you have tried and are convinced that this is effective, you won't worry about where the next gain is going to come from; you know it's coming ("Anxious for nothing").

If you are unable to grasp this concept of giving, of allowing your wealth to flow through you instead of settling around you, your wealth may be very short-lived, or you will tend to waste and squander.

If you choose to try any or all of the suggestions and tips in this book, this is *the most important*. Take this piece of wisdom seriously and consider yourself a champion of financial freedom. If you choose to ignore anything outlined here, so be it; just don't let it be this principle. You need to give. **MOST IMPORTANTLY**: Give freely, but do not (under any circumstances) brag about or otherwise tell other people what you give, how much you gave, and to whom you gave. It is none of anyone's business. If you do, then you have already received your return in the form of the attention you get from boasting of your kindness and generosity. One more tip to the wise: when you write your checks for your monthly expenses, write these FIRST.

Secret #2: Take courses and attend seminars and workshops that keep you informed and current in the area of business and finances. Read books and magazines, listen to audiotapes and watch videotapes on building personal wealth and managing finances. You will find several common threads and universal principles in these resources. Education does not stop at graduation, especially in the ever-evolving area of finances. Try continuing education courses at local colleges, and adult education centers. Check out distance-learning courses offered on the Internet.

Be a lifetime learner. There are thousands of books and tapes at NO charge at local libraries and available for a nominal fee at bookstores. You should purchase books and tapes that are particularly helpful and eye opening for you so that you have them as reference. Tapes should be played repeatedly to reinforce what is being communicated.

There are several good educational television shows especially on public TV and interesting articles in the newspaper, but be careful. They [the media] are usually biased towards their sponsors and advertisers, so you may have to glean knowledge from these two sources. Remember no one person or organization has all the answers to building wealth or taking control of your financial situation. No one method or group of suggestions works all the time for everyone in getting out of debt and on the right road to saving and investing for your future. There is no **easy** path or shortcut to gaining wealth, so read and absorb as much as you can to keep yourself focused on what you are accomplishing.

Increase your awareness of uncommon and innovative investment strategies and sources of income such as real estate tax-lien certificates, tax deeds, reverse mortgages for seniors, flipping real estate, and rental property management. Develop an understanding of stock options and futures. Just don't overdo it by becoming obsessed, confused or ill advised. Remember, the ignorant, naive, and uninformed are prime bait for shysters and scam artists. So empower and shield yourself against them through education.

What works well for many, in terms of learning about investing and the stock market, is to join an investment club. Members of a club have the benefit of the combined knowledge (and funds) of its participants, and they share in the earnings and participate in the decision-making process in terms of what investments to trade. Members can include family, friends, business associates, or all of the above. The best resource for information on starting an investment club is the National Association of Investors Corporation (NAIC) at 877-275-6242. Their web site at www.better-investing.org has educational materials and good evaluation and research tools.

Many people become financially fit and secure over time, simply because of the unavoidable lessons life teaches as we traverse the roads toward maturity (e.g. live and learn). But we can hasten reaching this coveted milestone by being open to learning and keeping up-to-date on the many aspects of personal and business financial management.

Secret #3: Watch the wealthy and do what we do. Emulate successful people. Observe what we do [and don't do] and adopt some of the good habits. Pay attention to people who invest in their children through useful tools like laptop and desktop computers, books, encyclopedias, investment vehicles, travel, cultural events, and any other items that contribute to their educational growth and financial stability. In my opinion, people who are insecure tend to spend lavishly on material possessions like clothes, jewelry, and cars. There is certainly nothing wrong with owning nice things, [I have a few myself] and we should want only the best, if for no other reason than quality lasts longer. But all major purchases have to be kept in perspective.

There are several books that document behavior patterns of the wealthy. The findings might surprise you. (See "Giving Credit Where Credit Is Due" at the end of this book). Study these books and learn from those who have achieved what you are seeking.

Not only will you learn and grow by surrounding yourself with successful people, but you should also watch and learn from yourself. Be your own biggest critic. Closely scrutinize your major moves and activities as they relate to finances, and try not to repeat the same mistakes. It is very important to learn from them and try not repeat them, if possible. Sometimes we need to repeat mistakes in order for the lessons they teach us to really sink in. But you will reach your goals much faster if you think about what you did wrong in one situation and commit not to do the same thing again when the same or similar situation arises.

Secret #4: Optimize. Let's discuss two areas that you can fully exploit to hasten reaching your financial goals: (A) Managing your finances; and, (B) Deciding where and how you live.

(A) Managing your finances. For couples, if both partners are financially savvy, that's great. You can divide responsibilities of managing the finances between you. If one of you is challenged in this area, let the one who best knows how to manage the finances, do so. Many marital problems stem from mismanagement of money. If you are contemplating marriage or beginning to commit to a long term relationship, consider requesting copies of both your credit ratings, sit down and plan how the finances will be structured, and decide who will do what. Some people enjoy record keeping, planning, and managing funds. But everyone is not good at paying bills, balancing checkbooks, saving, investing, tracking expenditures, and all the bookkeeping that comes along with life. Both partners MUST understand how to manage finances, but one of you should take a leadership role in carrying out the responsibilities. Couples should discuss this and let the bean counter maintain the books, or at least share in the tasks.

Consider at least one joint account where both of you can write checks or otherwise access funds. Obviously, financial decisions such as major purchases and establishing financial goals will require input and consensus from both partners.

Financial fitness and personal money management must be a team effort. If both of you are financially challenged, seek outside help. There are many no cost and low cost counseling and financial planning options available to you. If you obtain a large sum of money and are not confident that you know how to manage it, or just don't feel confident about how to manage finances in general, hire an advisor. The cost you pay up front may save you lots of money in the long run. These professionals can show you how to manage your day-to-day finances, provide suggestions on investment strategies, and suggest legal means to reduce your taxes. Exercise extreme care in selecting these individuals, making sure you choose someone who is objective, not a salesperson pitching his/her products.

Here are several tips to consider when selecting a financial planner, advisor, or consultant: (1) Ask how they are compensated: whether they are paid by commission, hourly, or fee based. This is important because a few commissioned professionals merely sell you products like mutual funds or insurance policies, may refer you to lending institutions which pay them considerable fees at your expense, or convince you to participate in specific funds which benefit them more than you. (2) Find out whether they follow up with you after their initial consultation and recommendations, and whether there are ongoing or continued fees for this service. A good financial plan should include some type of regular review of your portfolio. Why? Because your situation changes, the stock market and overall economy fluctuates. It makes sense to review your portfolio regularly to make sure that it's diversified and balanced to match your personal and economical needs. (3) Be especially cautious if all their services are offered for "free" since nothing in life is truly free. Only the initial consultation should be free of charge. The initial consultation should explain the basic financial planning process and consist of a detailed information exchange to learn about your health, debt and other major responsibilities (do you care for elderly parents), and your existing financial plan and status. The next step involves performing an analysis of your information, providing advice or proposals for your review, and implementing your decisions. (4) If they do recommend products or services that will cost you, find out if they have used any of these services themselves. Look for a professional who is prosperous, who has taken his/her own advice, and is well on their way or is where you want to be. Ask for references of people he/she has helped. Some of the best financial professionals are found through word of mouth recommendations from people you trust, and who have seen positive results. (5) Make sure the professional is properly credentialed and engages in some type of ongoing or continuing education to stay current with the evolving changes in the financial arena. (6) Evaluate more than one potential professional, but don't overdo it by screening too many.

(B) Optimize where and how you live. Live within your means. It makes more sense to live comfortably with funds to save and invest, rather than to live check to check, on the edge, trying to maintain an image. If you have a steep mortgage payment and are heavy in credit card debt, or underinsured, or have no significant investments and savings, you may be headed for disaster. You should be able to purchase a good home at substantially less per month, and use that extra cash towards sensible financial expenditures and investments such as education and retirement. You do not have to drive the latest model car if it means a hefty monthly outlay, especially if you do not have adequate funds tucked away for emergencies and major purchases we all face. Sometimes sacrificing a few minor options during your major purchases such as an automobile, or holding onto to it a while longer after it's paid for can mean substantial savings for you in the long run.

Secret #5: Minimize your tax bill. Begin by investing in a reputable tax consultant at best or tax preparation software at a minimum. If you insist on preparing your own taxes that's fine. Just do your homework by educating yourself on the tax laws.

A tax consultant can pay off enormously in the long run as he or she knows numerous methods of legally cutting your tax bill. Going into detail here would be beyond my scope, but here are a few examples to whet your appetite: Did you know that under certain circumstances, you can deduct tax preparation fees (even the cost of tax preparation software), charitable contributions of cash, donated items, and moving and job hunting expenses? You may also be able to lessen your tax bill by selling losing securities at year end to offset capital gains taxes, hire your children if you're in business for yourself, and deduct savings bond interest if the bonds are used for tuition. Certain Individual Retirement Account contributions and withdrawals, alimony, small business losses, and even expenses associated with volunteer work may be deductible.

Some travel expenses are deductible if you engage in business during the trip. If your employer requires you to wear uniforms (which cannot be worn for general purposes) you may be able to take a deduction for them. There are other employment related expenses which may be deductible. Also, if you sell your principal residence, you may be able to avoid paying taxes on the gains from the sale. If you are pursuing higher education, you may be eligible for certain tax credits, and if you are a diversified investor, some of your T-bills or municipal bonds may be tax exempt, if used for higher education. Ask your tax preparer about these, they should certainly be able to explain them and how they may relate to your situation.

A good tax preparer, accountant, or attorney can explain all of these possibilities, show you ways to avoid or survive an audit, and more. Be prepared to put some time into gathering the requested records and interacting with your chosen professional to optimize your benefits. You have to be completely up front and open with this person. You need to be able to tell him/her absolutely everything you do [no matter how private] that could be directly or indirectly related to finances. No matter how miniscule or insignificant it may seem to you, your advisor may be able to legally turn it into a benefit for you. Make sure the person is credentialed, has adequate experience, and is willing to spend the time required to serve you properly, which may include accompanying you to an audit, if necessary. This is truly an area where you get what you pay for, so again, do your homework.

The government encourages certain behavior by allowing "tax breaks" or deductions to those who engage in this desired behavior. The tax code is written to foster conduct which results in generating revenue for the government and contributing to the economic base. For instance:

(A) The most obvious example is the deduction of interest on a home mortgage which encourages home ownership, resulting in not only your contributing to the tax base, but keeping cash flowing through the economic system via banks, contractors, and other professionals needed to maintain the home.

(B) Another example is your employment status. While gainful employment (working for someone else) is a benefit to the employee and employer, and contributes to the prosperity of all of us, business ownership is much more desirable as evidenced by the numerous tax breaks and deductions provided to small and big business owners.

There are many other behavioral characteristics that will benefit you in terms of taxation. All you need to do is learn about the tax laws, and/or find a competent professional who will minimize your taxes to your benefit.

If your tax situation is not complex, you may be able to have your taxes prepared and filed free of charge. Many low income, disabled, non-English speaking and elderly filers can use Internal Revenue Service (IRS) sanctioned VITA (Volunteer Income Tax Assistance) sites. IRS trained volunteers are there to help taxpayers prepare and file tax returns electronically. They accept forms 1040, 1040A, 1040EZ, and Schedules A & B. These sites are located at libraries, community centers, churches and even retirement homes. Call your local IRS office for a location close to you.

This well-kept secret of minimizing your tax situation, is key to building wealth, as it allows you to legally reduce your tax liability, thereby keeping more funds in your pocket for the short and long term.

Secret #6: Organize. To get and stay on track with a good financial plan, you must organize. Develop a system of record keeping that works for you. A personal computer is a must in this area; money management software is becoming more and more popular. Quicken© and Microsoft© Money are two of the industry favorites. Even if you own and use a computer, you still need a practical paper system of record keeping. Organize your records in a file cabinet or in desk drawers. Keep things like paid bills, receipts, warranties, cancelled checks, etc. Try to keep them in some kind of order, by date and preferably by type of record. For example, you can have folders representing specific items: insurance records, employment records and pay stubs, warranties, mortgage, pets' records, auto and home maintenance, bank, credit card, and brokerage statements, personal records, health and medical records, etc. If you itemize your deductions consider filing tax related records according to their tax deduction category (contributions, medical expenses, investment income, mortgage interest, home improvement, property tax records, etc.).

Try to develop your own system in a fashion that will allow you to find specific items when you need them. Separate permanent records folders from those you need to access often. Once a year (preferably after tax preparation) records for the previous year should be grouped and labeled for that year and stored for at least 5 years. Get into the habit of doing this and it will become second nature.

In order to stay on top of paying your bills on time, you will need a daily filing system and a monthly routine of doing this. It may be completely manual, or a combination of manual and automated (computerized) solutions. For example, most of my bills are paid through automatic deductions from a checking account or through an online bill paying service (that's the geek in me). But I still have a few that I prefer paying manually through the mail. I have an envelope holder where I store bills to be paid. As I open my mail, I carefully examine each bill to ensure my last payment was credited properly, that the balance has been updated accordingly, purchases (if any) are accurate, interest (if applicable) has been calculated properly, and, note the due date of the next payment.

In the lower right-hand corner of the envelope, I write a date 5 days prior to the date the bill is due and place it in the holder where the next earliest date is visible. I glance at this holder on a daily basis noting the next due date. To minimize the number of times I have to sit down and write checks, I review any existing bills in the holder and try to target the pay date close to the most recent ones. I am careful to allow enough time for the mail to arrive on time, and for me to walk around a day or two with the bill in my briefcase or in the car visor waiting to be mailed. If you really dislike the check-writing task, try to do it during your peak performance time of day, not when you are tired, stressed or otherwise winding down after a busy day.

This system has worked well for me. You should develop your own system that does not make the check writing task a nuisance. Keep stamps and envelopes near the bills so you won't have to go on a treasure hunt when it's time to write checks. Pre-address envelopes to organizations that don't provide return envelopes.

A word about priorities: Your common sense tells you that basic needs such as the roof over your head (mortgage/rent) is more important than a manicure or hair style, and having electricity flowing to your home is more significant than having cable TV or cellular service. Think twice before buying a new outfit if you are a little short and your car payment or insurance is due.

If you get into a bind and need to decide who gets paid first, (after you pay yourself), understand that most merchants have contracts with credit agencies, where they provide monthly updates. A 30-day late payment is very hard to explain or clear once it's on your record. Don't put off the nonessential bills too long, they also will go through collection agencies to recover debt.

Organization is a very important key to becoming and remaining financially sound. Wealthy individuals know where they stand, and can usually put their hands on important records and documentation when needed. Here are a few key items that should *always* be readily available, but protected from theft, fire or water damage. Consider renting a safe deposit box to hold them:

- A copy of your Last Will & Testament and Medical Power of Attorney
- A list of credit card account numbers with their expiration dates, issuer name, and toll free telephone numbers to report theft or fraud
- An inventory of everything in your home including photos or a video tape of every room
- Savings Bonds, CD's, Stock & Bond Certificates (Keep a record of their serial numbers separate)
- Insurance policies, Adoption papers, your passport
- Mortgage documents, Deeds and Titles
- Birth, marriage, and death certificates
- Divorce decree, prenuptial agreement

Secret #7: Party. Have fun with your newly found knowledge and attitude about financial fitness. Never get so serious and wrapped up in anything that you forget how to have a good time. Don't allow yourself to get so driven that you lose track of what is really important (enjoying your life). You won't get to live your life a second time.

Play as hard as you work. Struggle to find that *balance* between working sensibly towards a comfortable tomorrow, yet slowing down long enough to smell the roses today. Treat yourself, your partner and your children. Vacation often: Take your spouse on one and the entire family on another, or go away alone to be with your thoughts, loosen up, and plan your next moves. Do whatever it takes to relax.

Learn to appreciate humor and let out a good laugh. Find out what entertains you to the point of a good belly laugh and indulge yourself in it as often as possible. Laughing is healthy. Being able to see the lighter side of life is good for us. Visit your local comedy clubs, rent a funny movie, read a humorous novel, repeat any good jokes you hear. Seize every opportunity to be entertained where you can laugh at yourself and all the funny things that happen in our daily lives.

Indulge yourself by doing what YOU enjoy. Try to be spontaneous, take a day off (use discretion) from your job or business and do what pleases YOU. Treat yourself to a relaxing massage and pedicure. Some spas offer packages where they give you (male or female) the works for a day. Aren't you worth it? In some states professional, licensed masseurs make house calls; try them. Especially when you see your debt start to shrink and your financial portfolio begins to grow. Go for it!

Try those secrets. When they begin to work for you, pass the word on to family and friends.

TWELVE THINGS I WISH I HAD KNOWN TWENTY YEARS AGO

It took many years for me to get to the point where I could honestly say, "I have no regrets." If I had all of my years to repeat, I would not change the order or paths I took, because I may not have evolved into the person I am today. But like you, I am human and from time-to-time tend to reflect back on the years, wishing I had an edge by learning something before it was time for me to learn it. The era when I was most naive was during my early to mid twenties; I thought I knew everything about everything. Years later, I would admit I knew absolutely nothing. I am describing results of these reflections, hoping you will benefit from some of the "common sense" knowledge I have gained over the years.

1. I wish I had known that the company I kept (personal and business associates) had a great deal to do with the direction my life took. I was fortunate to have many positive role models around who taught, encouraged, and guided me in the right direction. Avoid people who discourage you, tear you down, doubt your abilities, or exhibit negative attitudes. Consider adopting a mentor who will serve as a positive influence in terms of managing finances and building wealth. Make sure the person is knowledgeable, disciplined, and demonstrates honesty

and integrity in all areas especially how he/she handles their finances. A mentor must be able to educate, guide, constructively criticize or genuinely praise you, and most importantly, the person must be wise enough to know when each is appropriate.

2. I wish I had known to take the initiative to understand interest and how it works. The magic of time and compounding interest works in our favor, but credit card interest and minimum payments can literally keep you in debt and bondage for life. There is detailed information on the Internet on all forms of interest, finance charges, and all of the associated benefits and setbacks (see Appendix C). Ask your financial advisor, counselor or broker for additional information. The bottom line is wealthy people earn interest, everyone else pays interest.

3. I wish I had known the effectiveness of planning and setting goals, and that establishing, then concentrating on realistic goals keeps you focused and prepares you for future events such as a college education. For example, saving for an education can be more advantageous than going into debt by borrowing to finance it. Educational loans have delayed many parent's retirements and set families back several years, simply because they had not planned for the expense of an education. Scholarships and grants should be pursued, but certainly should not be relied

upon. There are other options to be considered in planning for educational expenses. Some are sanctioned by the government. For example, there are tax incentives associated with college savings plans. The Economic Growth and Tax Relief Reconciliation Act of 2001 allows federal tax exemption on earnings from state college savings plans, when the funds are used to pay for the following higher education expenses: tuition, room and board, books and fees, and other expenses that students pay to attend any qualified college or university in the United States.

Practically every state has implemented innovative college savings plans designed to meet the savings needs of just about everyone. These plans are sometimes referred to as "Qualified State Tuition Programs," or "Section 529 plans," named after the section of IRS code that covers them. They are sanctioned at the federal level, which gave states flexibility to contrive and tailor programs that best meets the needs of its citizens. As stated, the federal government provides tax exemption for the plans, and allows states to provide additional tax benefits at their level.

Two types of plans are **prepaid** tuition arrangements and educational **savings** accounts. I mention them here because of the potential financial benefit to anyone who is interested. Covering them in detail would require an entire chapter and could easily fill a book, but here are a few highlights: The prepaid arrangement essentially allows you to lock in today's tuition rates for an education down the road. The funds are invested and can be contributed via lump sum or monthly payments.

The savings accounts allow you to save money on behalf of an individuals higher education expenses (even your own). Some offer a variable rate of return; some guarantee a minimum rate of return. Account specifics will vary by state, but here are a few particulars which may be included: Account funds can be used nationwide at eligible educational institutions. Contributions can be made via check, cash, money order, and even credit card. Other family members and friends can contribute to the account and their gifts could qualify for tax breaks. If the beneficiary later chose not to use the money, the creator of the account can designate a new beneficiary, usually with no adverse tax consequences. There is annual rollover capability from one qualified program to another. Many states have plans that are open to residents of other states.

If you need to save for college, these plans are worth exploring. They can help you prepare for the cost, and save and earn money during the process. This is something that really needs to be well thought out because there are so many plans with many features. Settling on the right one will depend on your individual requirements and goals. Ask your financial advisor or planner for details or start with this website www.collegesavings.org for more information. You can also search for "529 plan" using your favorite search engine on the internet, or visit your local library and grab a book outlining the basics.

4. I wish I had known the value of a good credit rating, and how much your credit history impacts your credit future. I had no idea how much credibility, respect and true power came along with a good credit report, when shopping for a car or home. I didn't know how personally enriched I would feel knowing I had the integrity, honor, and state of mind that comes along with a good reputation in both the personal and financial arenas as evidenced by a reputable credit report.

You should request a copy of your credit report at least once a year to confirm its information. Obtain an understanding of how creditors rate you. Most use a point system based on specific factors in your current financial standing and past credit history. Sometimes these scores are referred to as your BEACON, EMPIRICA, or FICO scores, and are computed based on the details in your current credit report. The score changes as your profile changes. Many lenders use this score as one method to estimate the level of risk connected with a person's application for credit. The higher the score, the lower the risk. People with high scores have proven to repay debt in a more timely and consistent manner. Other evaluation criteria may include the length of time your accounts have been open, your balance/available credit ratio, the number and kinds of accounts in your name, and most importantly, payment history. Informed consumers have caught on to this and stay aware of what information is maintained in their credit files.

Don't get tricked by expensive credit repair companies or people who claim to be able to wipe a bad report clean. Some are legitimate, but many are pure scams. You created the situation, so you should take responsibility and the time to legally clean it up yourself. If information is correct, it cannot be removed until the designated timeframe elapses (commonly 7 years from the date of last activity). You can usually have incorrect information removed or corrected by simply writing a letter to the creditor and reporting agency. To rebuild bad credit, make agreements with creditors you owe and lay out a plan to pay them back. Sooner or later you will HAVE TO BORROW money. Don't expect to achieve financial success if you are unable to borrow, and don't expect to be able to borrow if you have a poor credit rating.

5. I wish I had known that the stock market was not just for a choice few, nor was it complicated and involved. I wish I had known that anyone could get into the stock market with a small amount of money to begin with. I had no idea that more than 500 companies had dividend reinvestment programs, and direct investment programs, where investors can buy as little as a single share of stock directly from them without going through a broker, then buy more on a regular basis in an amount suitable to their financial situation. Some companies have minimums to start with ($25 to $250), but many have none, and most are reputable successful companies. Today, stock trades can be executed directly online for as little as $10 per trade by opening a brokerage account. Some have low monthly fees, with no minimum balance requirements. Detailing this one is beyond the scope of this book, but well worth researching. Go to your local library (or search the Internet) and obtain general information on investing in the stock market or information on companies with direct investment plans. Get started today. Better yet, seek the advice of a competent broker.

6. I wish I had recognized the importance of living within my means instead of insecurely and immaturely trying to keep up with the Joneses or impress friends and family by spending way beyond what I could afford. Years of hard lessons taught me

not to spend on impulse and to avoid indulging myself when I really couldn't afford to. Small sacrifices back then could have meant obtaining financial fitness so much sooner.

7. I wish I had been made aware of the importance of maintaining ALL major types of insurance. Life, Health, Renter's, Fire and Theft, Auto, Home Owners, Title, Business, Disability, Long Term Care, Umbrella, etc. **ALL ARE KEY PROTECTIVE SHIELDS AND PREVENTIVE MEASURES TO AVERT FINANCIAL RUIN.** What may seem to be an insignificant expense in terms of keeping the premiums paid, could keep you and your family out of a major financial crisis. How many newscasts have you seen where an unsuspecting family lost all their belongings due to fire, theft, or accident, and had no insurance to replace them? Lack of adequate life insurance can result in causing the deceased to be put to rest with little or no dignity, or impose undue burden on friends and family members who may have to exhaust savings or go into debt to cover their loved ones final expenses. Get some life insurance, and get it now. Because the older you get, the more expensive the premiums will be.

Many business owners have become bankrupt or sued for their personal assets, because they were not properly insured and protected. In many of these cases, the responsible (or irresponsible) individual was aware of the benefits of insurance, but simply chose to ignore it as a priority, putting their funds elsewhere until it was too late. Don't let this happen to you. If you are physically able to earn an income, to support yourself and your family, be intelligent enough to realize no one is invulnerable and everyone is susceptible to accidents, mishaps, and tragedy. Be prepared; insure! That old axiom really applies to insurance: "I would rather have it and not need it, than to need it and not have it."

8. I wish I had known what a financial rip-off some of those extended warranties and service contracts were. I agree it makes sense to "buy" peace of mind by covering yourself with insurance for emergencies. But most of those service contracts they try to sell you on new purchases are purely money gobblers designed to make more dough for the manufacturers and retailers. If the product is worth your hard-earned funds, it should include a decent warranty and should [with proper use] function well beyond the warranty period. Instead of buying the service contract, put what you would pay in service contract fees in the bank annually, and use it to pay for service if it is ever needed. If it is not needed for service, use that cash to spend on something else, (you).

9. I wish I had known how easy it is for banks to make mistakes. Recent studies revealed a large percentage of Americans do not balance their checkbooks. Yikes! That's like playing Russian Roulette with your finances every month. I used to work at two major Maryland banks, in the department where checks and deposit tickets were coded for eventual input into the computer. Human beings keyed in those scan codes on the bottom of your checks and deposit tickets that were eventually run against the computer to debit and credit your account. Flawed, error prone human beings keyed those in. A $100 dollar check can easily be erroneously coded and debited from your account as a $1000 check. One errant zero can send your checks bouncing for weeks, with you having to suffer great agony and frustration [and fees] before it's all straightened out. I am sure there are better verification mechanisms in place now, but with human beings involved, anything is possible.

In recent years, I recall media stories where many depositors found unauthorized withdrawals from their accounts. This convenient method of debiting [a demand draft] comes in handy for making business transactions over the telephone, but has been recently abused by some unscrupulous telemarketers and scam artists. A close review and monthly balancing of your checkbook is a good measure and should catch such errors.

Many banks will show you **how to balance your checkbook** at no cost to you. Learn how to balance it and get into the habit of doing it regularly. It's your money that's at stake. See Appendix A for a quick and easy way to balance your checkbook.

10. I wish I had known what "caveat emptor" meant. I wish I had realized that if it sounds too good to be true, it most likely is too good to be true. I refuse to tell you how many "quick," "easy," and "fast" wealth building or money-saving endeavors I tried when I was too young and naïve to realize that nothing is FREE. Nothing comes without a price, and nothing that is worthwhile having comes overnight. Make sure you take the time to fully investigate any idea that is presented to you that will cost you money. Even when you achieve wealth, if you want to keep it, you must be mindful in this area.

Beware of multi-level marketing approaches. Many of them are legitimate, but some only build wealth for those who concocted the plan in the first place. For example, in my opinion, many infomercials are carefully constructed to appeal to our basic need of security, and our desire for an "easy" and inexpensive way to wealth. They capitalize on our weakness by painting pictures of dream homes, expensive cars, people relaxing on a quiet beach as they sit back and count all the money that supposedly rolls in from whatever magical program the sponsors are selling.

The convincing is not complete without testimonials (some legitimate, I'm sure), from "people just like you" who have made it using their system. There have been so many people who have been victimized over the years, and have formally complained, there are now regulations that require additional disclosure. So watch for fine print at the bottom of your television screen, or record it so that you can slowly and repeatedly listen to the fast talk where subtle warnings are sometimes provided.

Beware of any business transaction where the initiator or seller insists you must act immediately. Question deals where you are told you must "sign now," or "buy today." Always question; why the urgency? You should always be given the opportunity to investigate anything that is going to cost you money. You should never deny yourself the opportunity to clear your head and step outside of pressure situations where you might be forced to buy or commit prematurely. You can then take the time to rethink and investigate major decisions without procrastinating.

Do your homework before falling for rebates. Many manufacturers know that most people will never take the time to mail in rebate forms. Even if it is not the mail-in type of rebate, if it is a substantial amount involved, usually as part of a package deal, you can be assured that the cost is almost always factored into some other part of the deal. Look for the fateful asterisk and read the fine print. This could result in keeping hundreds of dollars in your pocket.

Pyramids are illegal in many states, so some innovative individuals have restructured them into programs that appear legitimate. Throughout this book, you will find I have promoted the use of the Internet because of the vast amount of information out there. But again, because of its far reaching capability, it is also a playground for many such schemes. Probably more so because the business, individual, or company is sight unseen. Use the Internet wisely, but like anything else, you need to investigate and confirm everything, especially when it comes to your hard-earned dollars.

Beware of the old deceptive unbundled pricing technique. This is where you are shopping for the best deal, find what you believe is the best price, only to learn of additional unrevealed charges when you go to make the purchase. Some vacation packages were advertised in this manner. Automobiles and the cost of tires used to be advertised like this. Laws have been enacted and agencies are in place to keep us informed and protect us against such practices (e.g. the Federal Trade Commission or the Better Business Bureau).

11. I wish I had known that I needed to plan for retirement. I would have started saving and investing earlier. I did not seriously start to think about retirement until I hit age 35. If I had started ten or fifteen years earlier, the fortune I could have amassed is mind-boggling. The sooner you get started planning, saving and investing for retirement the better off you will be, but it is never too late to start. If you have a pension plan or retirement account on your job, ask for an estimate of how much it will pay. This will provide a dose of reality and could indicate a need to obtain or plan for additional income. **_Reality Check_**: You should check your Social Security records every year to confirm that your earnings are being reported properly. As of this writing, workers are **automatically** sent a copy of their Social Security Statement annually, about three months before their birthday.

Ask your financial advisor or broker about *tax exempt* and *tax-deferred* investment strategies for retirement. Again, there is no one size fits all strategy. The best vehicle for you will depend on many things, such as your age, financial situation, marital status, etc. You will be pleasantly surprised to learn how much these strategies can benefit you today and in the future.

The best thing you can do for yourself is plan NOW by first imagining yourself as retired. Write down what you plan to do (travel, work part time, engage in hobbies, volunteer, etc.). Estimate how much income you will receive, where it will come from, and for how long. Estimate your expenses during retirement. **THIS IS EXTREMELY IMPORTANT.** Although many current expenses will be alleviated, they will be replaced with new ones. Take time to list every expense you expect to have when retired. People are living longer. Two things that will be very difficult to estimate are health care expenses and inflation. So be sure to include adequate insurance and funds for continued saving and investing. Most people will find they need about 75% of their pre-retirement income to live comfortably. Once you have an idea of your income and expenses, you can plan for any additional income you may need to maintain an enjoyable lifestyle.

12. I wish I had known how exhilarating it would be to learn about the many aspects of the financial arena, such as investment vehicles, loan types, savings and checking account types, banking rules and regulations, and real estate laws and guidelines. Hopefully, you too will learn that obtaining

knowledge, which results in putting and keeping you on the right track, is fun. I never knew how enjoyable and rewarding it would feel to have peace of mind in controlling my finances. To me, this is the true meaning of wealth, being "above only" by being able to obtain whatever is desired, and not having to worry about anything.

One word of caution; take your time. As you learn, invest, and begin to see financial gains, you may get excited and become tempted to seek "instant" and "quick" investment strategies or wealth building methods. I know I certainly did. But remember, there are no short cuts to wealth. You must learn about the many basic aspects of the financial world before moving on to the next phases. Don't forget the charlatans who tap into our eagerness to "have it now." They have clever ways of making us think we can side-step basic required learning processes and passage of time, and jump straight into the big league. Use every bit of self control and discipline you can muster to ignore such promises.

WHERE DO WE GO FROM HERE?

Financial fitness, like any fitness program, is a lifelong undertaking. Throughout this process, you will want to stay informed and stick with your plan. As you get older, marry, as your children mature and move on, your needs will change and so should your plan. **Review your plan and adjust your goals as your life experiences dictate.**

But what about after you're gone? Do you have a responsibility to plan beyond retirement? Absolutely; especially if you have family or other loved ones who need to be considered. This is commonly referred to as *Estate Planning* and should also be part of any smart wealth-builder's plan. Wealthy people of integrity have enough forethought to pass on sound wealth building principles AND an inheritance to their heirs. This is all part of sowing and reaping, obtaining enough to enjoy a hearty healthy life, with plenty invested and left over to leave to your successors, who will hopefully use it wisely and pass it on to their heirs.

Unless you have gone through it, most people don't have a clue as to what needs to be done to settle an estate when one dies. There are financial debts (the deceased's bills) that must be paid and closed, state and federal taxes to be paid, and several types of property to distribute.

Laws and policies regarding probate vary from state to state. If you don't adequately plan for dissemination of your assets, by indicating in writing your wishes after graduating this life, it is highly likely that you will subject others to severe financial hardship and headaches. You can expect family squabbles as to who gets what, including disposition of your children, and unnecessary probate fees and taxes, all through a protracted painstaking and stressful legal process. Getting an understanding and planning for them NOW can avert these mishaps.

First, you will want to start with a will. Set up an appointment with an attorney to discuss the types of wills, trusts, and other avenues available to you for estate planning. They can recommend legal ways to cost effectively and intelligently pass on wealth according to your desires. For example, you may have children to whom you have not been able to impart sound financial habits, but being the good parent that you are, you still want to include them in your will. There are ways you can leave them a distribution over time, so they won't just run through or otherwise squander any lump sum.

A good will is appropriate for most estates, but you should also familiarize yourself with living trusts and decide whether one makes sense for you. These can provide a means of protecting your property now, and saving your beneficiaries exorbitant probate fees later.

Don't want to bother with an attorney? That's fine too. There is impressive inexpensive computer software that can create a legal will in an hour or so. All you need is the basic information on the individuals and organizations that you want to mention in your will. Decide who you want to handle your affairs when you're gone. Plan for how you want your wealth distributed and outline it in a will, by either buying the computer software and be done with it, or by visiting a professional who can do it for you.

You now have a good foundation and an arsenal of information to help you stay informed and make changes as needed. There are a host of good resources in the bookstores, public libraries, and especially on the Internet that will help you stay focused and provide more detail on any topic outlined in this book.

Congratulations! If you have gotten this far, you are obviously not one to whine and complain about your situation or wait for a magical solution to drop from the sky. You are proactive and diligent. You realize that you have to take action and stay the course to improve your situation. You have done so by beginning the process of educating yourself on why you should be "above only", and how to become "anxious for nothing." You are smart enough not to flaunt, boast or brag about your wealth. You realize that it is more intelligent to be confident yet discreet about your assets. In the long run, this may help you protect them. You understand key wealth building principles, which will help you accumulate and maintain wealth by controlling spending, reducing debt, saving, investing, and estate planning. Meanwhile you can enjoy the abundance of all that's available to you in the process.

A FEW FINAL FINANCIAL DO'S & DON'TS

Here are a few more common sense guidelines which may help you reach your financial goals, properly structure your finances, and maintain the wealth you are able to accumulate.

- **Do** invest in a computer for your home and business. Include Internet access and financial management software, at a minimum. There are unlimited volumes of information on every topic imaginable on the World Wide Web. *You Give Your Family And Business A Competitive Edge By Purchasing A Computer And Connecting To This Invaluable Resource Known As The Internet.* Financial management software can simplify your money management tasks and provide excellent records to help you organize, plan, manage and control your financial endeavors. Many companies that produce such products have related websites loaded with information at no cost. Tax preparation software can make tax time much more tolerable. Most of them work by simply asking a series of questions, then preparing the necessary forms and schedules based on your responses. Some of them even link to your financial software so most of the information is already readily available keeping you from having to hunt for it.

Major government organizations which we all have to deal with have kept pace with technology. The best example of this is the IRS. For some unknown reason they have figured out how to efficiently and cost effectively allow us to use our computers for electronic filing of our taxes. More informed taxpayers are taking advantage of this service as it has proven to be reliable, fast, and secure. Most reputable tax preparation businesses support and recommend electronic filing for their clients who qualify.

Nearly all desktop and laptop computers come equipped with a variety of other useful software programs. I've listed a few of samples below:

A) Database management software used for tracking name and address contact information; some automatically dial the telephone number with the click of a mouse.

B) Word processing software with built-in dictionaries and encyclopedias. The word processing obviously contributes to better record keeping. You will be able to store and find documents efficiently and quickly.

C) Internet browser software used to surf the Internet. You will need to obtain access through an Internet Service Provider.

If you include access to the Internet, you can download more useful software for free. For example, you can download savings bond tracking programs which automatically calculate interest, and financial calculators which automatically amortize and calculate interest and payment information on all types of loans. Every reputable stockbroker has a website, and many offer delayed and real-time stock quotes, detailed stock and mutual fund research information, real time trade capability, which are usually lower than the cost of dealing directly with a broker over the phone.

Consider online banking and bill-paying services, especially if you dislike writing and mailing checks. There is obviously a cost associated, but it is usually nominal and the service itself is quite convenient. If your employer provides direct deposit, you may be able to arrange automatic payments into your savings, investments, or toward your bills.

A personal computer is no longer viewed as a luxury item; it is a necessity and can help you keep accurate records of all financial transactions. You will need the records for tax preparation, to resolve many kinds of disputes, and for your own personal tracking of your expenditures and income. Embrace technology; take advantage of its ability to save you time and money in your personal and business endeavors.

- **Don't** procrastinate; pay your bills on time! This is the first most important step towards maintaining a good credit rating and being "anxious for nothing." Credibility is crucial; remember, your children are watching you and will most likely pick up your spending and money management habits. Teach them about the financial world as early as possible. Put them on the right path by setting a good example. This is one way the affluent keep money in their families; they perpetuate good financial fitness habits by passing on valuable knowledge to their children.

Most people want a better life for their children, and this is understandable. But try not to overdo it or indulge them by overcompensating for what you did not have. Think about what you are doing to them by providing so much without properly teaching them the value of a dollar. You could be hindering them from learning valuable lessons if you continue to spoil them or "bail them out" of precarious financial situations. They could grow up thinking someone is always supposed to give and provide for them. Since they don't teach children about finances early enough in school, it is your responsibility to do this. Follow up your teachings by providing a good example. Start by paying your bills on time.

If you don't pay on time you will eventually have bad credit. If you have bad credit you cannot be "anxious for nothing." You will be fodder for sales people, creditors, and banks because you have no credibility on which to stand. With bad credit when you go to shop for a car, you may have to dicker and haggle with the dealer, waiting for him to run back and forth to his manager in an effort to wear you down (or up) to his price. You may have to sit there and sweat, hoping for a miracle, while he checks your credit history. With bad credit, you may have to jump major hurdles if you want to purchase a house, and may end up paying much more than the house is worth, and could be subject to paying higher interest rates.

With bad credit, you may have to struggle to find venture capital if you need money to start your own business or expand your existing business. The most powerful negotiating tool you have at your disposal in any business transaction is a good credit rating. So pay your bills on time. You can't make demands or realistic counter offers if your credit is shaky. If you have a good payment record and credit rating, you won't need lots of money down; the offers will come to you.

- **Do** try to gather several "eggs" for your retirement "basket". For example, there are pensions, annuities, IRAs, and our individual investments, all potential [and hopefully a combination of] sources of income for retirement. I believe Social Security was never intended to fully fund retirement. The original bill submitted to congress defined it as "...financial assistance assuring a reasonable subsistence..." To me, these key words indicate Social Security is meant to provide a marginal supplemental means of surviving, not a complete source of income.

- **Don't** be a bad risk; establish some credit in your own name. Both partners in a relationship must understand the basics of finances and each should have credit in his/her own name. I have observed on several occasions that after divorce, one partner's quality of life improves while the other partner's declines. Usually because one partner neglects to have some credit history of his/her own and ends up having to re-establish credit worthiness after divorce. If you are contemplating marriage seriously consider a prenuptial agreement. In the unlikely event, if something should happen, you will have clearly documented how certain assets will be allocated and one partner won't get taken to the cleaners.

- **Do** steer clear of costly "instant" tax refund deals; they charge significant fees and interest that would be best spent in your pocket. It has been noted that some unsuspecting tax payers received "loans" in the amount of their refunds from these companies. The tax payers later learned they would receive less of a refund than was originally anticipated, thus owing more on the loan (plus interest) to the tax preparer who provided the cash up front.

- **Don't** try to do everything yourself. Know when to solicit professional advice and services. You may be able to indirectly save more money (and your valuable time) by hiring professionals to do time consuming everyday tasks and chores: such as lawn service, maid or laundry service, pick up dry cleaning service, onsite pet grooming, and odd jobs around the house. Do the math, and if farming out certain tasks frees up more time for you to concentrate on your business and life outside of work, farm it out.

Staying informed is highly recommended and admirable. But in some cases it should just prepare and help you decide whether you need a professional. You must sometimes rely on the expertise of others who specialize in certain aspects of the financial arena, such as lawyers, brokers, real estate agents, financial advisors, tax specialists, pastors, counselors, and mentors. They have to eat too. Be prepared to pay a professional for what he or she is worth. Money doesn't always have to change hands. For example, you can be creative by considering bartering in addition to or instead of paying for services. Think of other (legal) alternative methods where you both win.

- **Don't** overdo it by repeatedly refinancing your home or borrowing against the equity in it. An equity loan or refinance can do wonders in terms of exchanging nasty credit card debt for good deductible mortgage debt. However, if taken to the extreme and abused, it could unnecessarily prolong paying off the mortgage. It might enable you to avoid disciplining yourself by controlling spending with those credit cards and other types of bad debt.

- **Do** consider the use of a charge card or debit card over a credit card. Where a credit card can get you into trouble if you have not conquered the urge to spend beyond your means, a charge card (payable monthly) or debit card (immediately deducts purchase costs from your account) tend to keep you in check, because you have to face the music and pay up, in the shorter term.

- **Don't** prepay static bills if you are trying to reduce debt. If you are paying off loathsome credit card bills, you need all the money you can get to do this as quickly as possible. Some people prepay bills where the full balance is due on receipt such as utility bills and recurring monthly bills. For example, I had a $10 cell phone bill which I often sent in $40-$50 to keep from having to write all those checks in small amounts. Pay the exact amount due in full; and use other funds to reduce debt.

- **Do** plan how you will fund your children's education while they are very young. Try not to wait until they are in high school before you think about where the funds will come from to pay for higher education. This should be a key part of every parent's goals list and financial plan. You should not rely on scholarships. If the youngster is fortunate enough to gain a partial or full scholarship, all the better; you then have those funds to apply to other goals.

- **Don't** consider bankruptcy unless all else has failed. A recent study has shown that over the past 5 years, over one million Americans per year have filed bankruptcy under Chapter 7 or 13. It should be used only as a last resort after every other option has been evaluated, tried, and proven unsuccessful. Seek competent legal professional advice on this. Although bankruptcy provides a fresh start, it may involve losing your possessions and may take several years to expunge.

If bills begin to back up and late payments get out of hand, talk to your creditors. They will usually work with you in compromising and agreeing to some method of repayment. I used to work for two banks, sold real estate and got to know several bankers, loan officers, and financial gurus. Believe me when I tell you, legitimate lenders do not want to take your property (foreclose or repossess), all they want is their money. Sometimes all it takes is a simple phone call explaining your situation or a sincere letter outlining payment arrangements, to avoid falling too far behind.

- **Do** try several ventures at once, if you are an entrepreneur. Be creative and bold. Have several irons in the fire. If one fizzles out and does not meet your expectations, you can concentrate on another while you regroup and decide how to handle the problematic one. Remember the 70's television sitcom "Green Acres?" The entrepreneur, Mr. Haney knew the value of diversification in business didn't he? Seek a business at which you excel and something that you enjoy doing.

If at all possible, **pursue ventures that provide residual income.** For example, you could try: (1) Buying, then renting real property (house, duplex, condo, garage, office building, or a tract of land). Anything above expenses is yours to spend or invest further. (2) Writing a book or articles on topics in which you have expertise. These can then be sold or licensed producing royalty income for life. The same goes for jokes, poetry, musical arrangements, or songs. Comedians, speakers, entertainers and their agents are always looking for new material. (3) Finding a way to market information specific to your profession (e.g., mailing lists, statistics, etc.) can yield substantial gains. We live in an information age where people are willing to pay for useful data. (4) Serving as a literary agent, where you represent writers and publishers. These folks collect sizable commissions and royalties based on the agreements with their clients. 5) Providing technical writing services, professional copy editing, or proofreading services. They are also in demand. (6) Inventing an original product or improving on an existing idea. It is not as difficult as most people may believe. If you are unable to fund the idea, you may be able to find an investor willing to fund it. Make sure you do your homework by developing a solid business plan that reflects how you will prototype, patent, mass produce, and market your product. You may be positioned to gain substantial advances and collect handsome royalties over time.

- **Don't** gamble. Be cautious with lotteries, racetracks and casinos. You have a better chance of getting struck by lightning twice on the same sunny day than you have of winning the lottery. Notice where most lottery machines and agents are concentrated. They are usually in neighborhoods of people who can least afford to gamble. Lotteries are designed to pump millions into state budgets, not into your pocket. Some states have gone as far as to draw several numbers in one day. Others have numerous types of "scratch offs," and many more have pooled their resources to provide mega jackpots to further entice the gambler. If you bet $1 per day on lottery numbers you could have saved $365 per year, plus the compounded interest on it, enough to pay off an annual expense. In 3 years you could have saved $1095+, enough to pay off a bill or invest in a Certificate of Deposit or a few shares of stock. If you play regularly, add up the total cost you spend on a dream, and think about what you could have done with that cash if you had paid yourself. Studies have indicated that people who win large sums of money in a lottery are usually no better off and are often worse off than they were before winning. I think this is simply because of their lack of knowledge and discipline on how to handle finances. If you can't manage a mediocre amount, chances are you will also mismanage millions. Therefore, educate yourself on how to control your finances and you will be prepared for any situation. Gambling is addictive when not kept in perspective. It is an addiction that seems to be extremely tough to conquer.

- **Do** open a checking account if you don't already have one. Believe it or not there are still many people who purchase money orders or pay bills in cash, because they do not want to be bothered with managing a bank account. This is highly discouraged. You must learn how to master something as simple as a checking account if you aspire to manage and control your money and your future.

Shop for a no-fee, interest bearing account, one that is federally insured. Many banks will require direct deposit or a minimum balance for no-cost checking. When you open the account, have the bank representative explain their policies and show you how to balance the account. The account will provide valuable records of your expenditures, come in handy around tax time, and show that you have the basic intelligence and patience to manage your own funds.

- **Don't** cosign for **anyone** under any circumstances without a thorough understanding of the impact. It is simply not a good practice and can destroy credit ratings, as well as good relationships. When you cosign for something, you are saying to the lender, "If this person does not pay you, I will." Forget all the so-called good reasons why you would cosign for a friend or family member and keep that statement in mind. Forget whatever reason they give you for asking you to sign. Put your personal feelings in your pocket, and be business-minded enough to say, "I am sorry; I cannot help you." Remember, the person asking for your signature can have all the good intentions of paying the debt on time. But bad things happen to good people and that person is no exception. Things may come up that are outside of his/her control, and he/she may have to make a decision to lower the priority of repaying the loan for which you signed. Enter trouble.

If you do decide to cosign, make sure you can afford to make the payments yourself. Because if the person you cosign for does not pay, the negative information can affect your credit rating. In some states, you could even be sued by the lender. If you put up property as collateral, such as a car, land or home, you could lose them if your borrower does not pay on time. To protect yourself, you could ask the lender to notify you if the borrower misses a payment. If that doesn't pan out, stay in touch with the borrower and periodically inquire as to the condition of the loan.

- **Do** maintain your automobile, your home, your clothes and other belongings in a manner which prevents costly repairs and premature replacement. If you neglect and abuse your car, you can be assured it will cost you in the long run. If you ignore basic maintenance of your dwelling, eventually you will have to spend much more on high-priced repairs and replacements. If you don't pay attention to specific garment cleaning instructions and manufacturer's maintenance directions on certain attire, you will constantly need to replace them.

- **Don't** keep secrets from your spouse or partner. Couples should reveal everything to each other at the onset of serious commitment and include each other in all financial activity. Secrets are destructive, will eventually reveal themselves, and could polarize you from your companion in terms of financial goals. Work together; pool your resources and strive to stay in accord, especially in the area of finances. Be honest in communicating with each other. Trust is extremely important. Integrity is everything.

- **Do** contribute the maximum to your company's retirement savings plan, if you can afford it, especially if your employer matches your contributions. This is yet another method of paying yourself first and minimizing your tax bill because many contributions come off the top before taxes are deducted. Unless you've been living on a distant planet you should have noticed that the U.S. Government has implemented (and is still implementing) incentives that encourage citizens to save for and invest in their own future. The most admirable of these incentives is the tax break and potential growth of the funds you contribute to retirement vehicles.

- **Don't** try to beat the tax man (the IRS) at his own game. It is simply not worth it and will not work. Remember integrity is everything and is key to being "anxious for nothing". There are many legal ways of cutting your tax bill, so that you only pay your fair share. So don't try to "get over" by cheating or otherwise trying to outfox uncle Sam. Pay your taxes on time. Procrastinating past the deadline, or not making estimated tax payments on time can cost you big bucks in unnecessary penalties and interest. By all means, don't take shortcuts. For example, if you are accustomed to taking the standard deduction on short forms, try the long form. Educate yourself on the tax regulations or hire a competent professional.

No one loves the IRS, I know I don't, but we all need to play by the rules. You will realize they are not unreasonable once you learn how the tax system is structured. If you do play by their rules, and just happen to get called in for an audit, it should not be a problem, because your mind is free of guilt and anxiety. All you'll need to do is produce the documentation to support your return.

- **Do** stay well within your credit limit on your credit card. Most companies levy fees for over-the-limit transactions. Remember, your goal is to reduce and eliminate credit card debt and maintain one card for emergencies. Avoid impulse buying by not taking your credit card and checkbook everywhere you go. For short local routine trips, leave home without them.

- **Don't** die intestate. Get a will and keep it current. If you die without indicating how your estate should be divided, your state law will dictate this. Many states have different [surprising] ways of doing this. You should not assume your spouse or children would be adequately provided for if you don't indicate such provisions while you are living. You can prevent family quibbles over who gets what by simply making your wishes known through a will. Unless you have a very complicated estate, most people can use computer software to generate a will. My recommendation is Willmaker© from Nolo.com Inc. for its ease of use, simplicity, and cost effectiveness. Their website is http://www.nolo.com.

- **Do** plan. When your financial situation gets to be very challenging and the outlook seems bleak, don't worry. Divert worrying time to planning time. Worrying will accomplish nothing and will tear you down emotionally and physically. It can make you overreact, panic, and do foolish things which disrupt your financial situation and derail your plans. Remember Joe's "R's": Relax, regroup, restructure your plan, and research information to find out what you need to do to take the next step towards attacking the problem and preventing it from recurring.

- **Don't** play around with child support funds. If things get rough and you need to temporarily restructure certain bills, this is not one to skip or take lightly. Not only do you have a moral responsibility to keep these payments current, but the law has become extremely intolerant and harsh on people who slack off on this commitment.

- **Do** protect your identity and personal information. Identity theft is rampant, and has caused major financial trouble for many people. Safeguard your mail by installing a mail slot in your door, renting a post office box, or purchasing a locking mailbox to prevent mail theft. Invest a few dollars in a good shredder, and with it, destroy all credit card offers, old bills, voided checks, and anything else that could identify you and your personal and business related information. There are criminals who actually weed through people's trash and garbage to find such items to use illegally. Never give out your credit card information, social security number, bank account numbers, or bank card personal identification number (PIN) to telemarketers or anyone you are not absolutely sure has a legal right or have them.

- **Don't** go shopping for a major purchase without doing your homework first. Check the Internet or your local library for materials to help you learn about the features and average costs of what you are looking to buy. If you go into a store not knowing what features or basic requirements you seek, some salesperson will surely make up your mind for you. This is the same as going grocery shopping without a list; you may come home with all sorts of junk and items bought on impulse, and still miss crucial staples that you needed. Most supermarkets are physically designed and laid out to make you buy on impulse.

- **Do** spend money wisely when giving gifts. Give gifts of cash, gift certificates for things your recipient enjoys, or gifts that promote good financial habits. For example, U.S. savings bonds, shares of stock, collectable coins, or financial related books and tapes. If you feel these things are inappropriate, at least give practical gifts people can use. Put some thought into it. For example, if you know your recipient does his/her own housework, give him/her a break by paying for a day or a week of maid service. If they have a newborn, buy them a few months of diaper service. If they tend to pamper their pets, pay for doggie day-care for a week or mobile pet grooming service. If they are worrisome or security conscious, get them a home security system, if they don't already have one. Use your imagination and stop giving cologne and toasters.

- **Don't** give up. As you take steps to improve your financial situation, don't give up *when* you hit a temporary setback or point of failure. Accept failures; don't deny them. Realize that setbacks are only temporary. Learn from them. When you fail, try that step again, try it differently, or use the failure as fuel to push you towards the next step in your plan.

In summary, remember the basics of obtaining wealth: Understand that you deserve to be financially fit; establish your short and long-term financial goals;

develop a plan that will allow you to reach those goals; know where your money goes by tracking expenditures; identify how much income you have to cover those expenditures; cut expenses and/or increase income to address the difference; and pay off bad debt, save, give, insure, invest, and periodically update your financial plan as your needs change.

The bottom line is to properly manage your finances with good common sense habits and techniques, yet spend enough to live and enjoy a healthy rewarding life. Consider and plan for the future, but enjoy the moment.

HOMEWORK, EXERCISES AND PROJECTS

These simple projects are intended to reinforce what has been already outlined. Try them at your convenience. Don't try to do them all at once, spread them out over time, and repeat them regularly. If you paid attention to the guidelines presented, the reasons will be obvious and the results may surprise you.

1. Become a mentor to a teenager. As you mature and succeed in your financial endeavors, teach him/her what you know. Develop projects and assignments to help them learn on their own. For example, have him/her identify basic elements of a credit/loan application. Obtain one from a bank or lending institution and examine it closely. Explain why each item is being requested to determine creditworthiness. Another example, take him/her to a bank and have them open a savings account. Or, when they are seeking topics for book reports or term papers, encourage them to consider financial topics. You could show them how to manage and balance a checkbook, or explain how an ATM debit card works and contrast it to how a credit or charge card works. Teach them how to read the financial section of the daily newspaper, or show them how to decipher the basic elements of a stock ticker.

2. Request your credit report. There are three major credit-reporting agencies. Go to the local library, the Internet, or the phone book and get the addresses and send your request [in writing] to each of them. If you are not squeamish about providing your credit card information on a secure website, you should buy it via the Internet (see Appendix C). The cost will be minimal, and you can get one for free if you have been recently turned down for credit. In many states you are allowed by law to get one complimentary report per year. When you get the copy, confirm everything contained in it is correct, and close out any inactive accounts by writing to the account holder. All credit reporting agencies include instructions on how to dispute items and correct misinformation.

3. Crunch up a dead president and plant that paper as a seed. Luke 6:38. This is a family tradition started by my brother years ago. I will never forget my reaction the first time he used it on me. Neatly fold or crumple up a $50 or $100 dollar bill (or more) and place it in the hands of someone you know. Approach them as if to shake their hand and simultaneously plant the seed in their palm. Tell them it's a treat, a gift, whatever you need to tell them in order to get them to accept it. Be careful whom you select so as not to send the wrong message (e.g. avoid any indications of intimacy or expectations of return; use common sense).

4. Try your luck and skill at picking stocks and mutual funds. Have some fun with this one. There are websites on the Internet that allow you to start with a pool of imaginary money to purchase stocks and/or mutual funds. (See Appendix C) There is no cost to do this exercise. Most sites include research tools, glossaries, and hoards of other information to educate you while you "play". There are literally thousands of websites packed with comprehensive information on the world of finances. Everything is available: learning about basics of investing; tracking stocks, bonds, and mutual funds; how to shop for the best rates on car and home loans; sample loan applications, small business training, financial plans, all kinds of calculators to help you fine tune your financial plan; and much more.

5. Buy lunch or dinner for a stranger without letting them know where it came from. Try this with elderly people or a young couple. If you visit a casual restaurant where you can do this without being detected, do it. Inform the waiter or cashier that you are just a friend. Pay their tab and leave.

6. Calculate your net worth. There are documents, books, magazines and Internet websites that show you how to do this. It is simpler than most people think and can aid in development and maintenance of your financial plan.

7. Support others generously. Invest in projects that family and close friends have undertaken. For example, if you have an acquaintance who is supplementing income by selling cosmetics or household items, support him/her by making a generous purchase. If you have a friend who has published a book, tape, or CD, buy several copies and give them as gifts. If you know someone who is an entrepreneur, support their business by patronizing it yourself. If he/she is reputable, refer family and friends to them as well. When people trust you with their business ideas, encourage them to pursue their dreams vigorously; offer to help where you can.

8. Register for a continuing education class in any aspect of finance. Local colleges and high schools often offer refresher courses in money management, investment strategies, home-based businesses, and a host of small business education courses. Get a friend to attend with you. Many offer discounts to senior citizens and some courses are even free of charge. If you feel you don't need any more education on finances, take a course on one of your favorite pastimes or hobbies.

9. If you live in an area where you sometimes have to shovel snow from your property and clean it off your automobile, remove snow from your neighbors property in addition to your own. If the neighbor is elderly, all the better.

10. Go on the Internet, using your favorite search engine, or visit your local library and research two very informative laws: the Equal Credit Opportunity Act and the Fair Debt Collection Practices Act. One has to do with your rights when you apply for credit; the other deals with what debt collectors can and cannot do in their collection practices. You should be familiar with both.

11. Volunteer to serve food to the needy at a local soup kitchen, halfway house, or other charity. Many allow volunteers to serve meals a few hours a day. If you cannot find one in your community, visit a nursing or convalescent home and ask to spend some time with residents who do not receive regular visits. If you can afford it, take it a step further and carry token gifts for the residents. For example, on Valentine's Day you could give a single rose to each female patient. Around the holiday season you could make grab bags and stuff them with staples and goodies that they all can use, such as lotion, toothpaste, soap, candy, fruit, large print books, magazines, etc.

12. Give yourself (and your family if applicable) an insurance check up. A good insurance agent should do this at no cost to you. List all the various types and amounts of insurance you currently carry, evaluate your situation based on your goals, and decide whether you need to drop any or buy more. We all

should be aware of the following types of insurance. How many of them are you familiar with? Life, health, disability, long term care, automobile, travel, home owners, renters, mortgage, road hazard, business, flood, hurricane, umbrella, and pet. One more tip regarding your insurance check up--make sure your agent is an independent agent. They have a wider range of possibilities available to them and stand a better chance of saving you money.

13. Clean out your closets. Call your favorite charity and donate all those clothes and shoes you've outgrown. In addition to giving things you know you don't want, donate something new or recently purchased, but in good condition. Get rid of all those knickknacks and keepsakes you've been stashing. Purge your attic and storage space. If you have something you have not used in a year, you don't need it. So get rid of it. If the organization you are donating to is a non-profit organization, get a receipt; you may be entitled to a tax deduction.

14. Show someone you are thinking about them. Don't wait for a holiday or special occasion to act. For single people, if you know a couple with children, volunteer to baby-sit while the couple enjoys a night on the town. The ideal gesture would be to buy them a gift certificate for dinner and a show and include a hand-drawn certificate to provide child care while

they're out. For married couples, if you know a single person who lives alone, invite him/her to breakfast, lunch or dinner. Try to prepare a meal you know he/she likes.

15. Go on the Internet or to your public library if you do not yet have Internet access at home. Learn who the following people are (some of my idols) and describe in 25 words or less their contribution to society, their philosophy, or simply their claim to fame: Warren Buffet, Suze Orman, John H. Johnson, Alan Greenspan, George Soros, Susan L. Taylor, Peter Lynch, Oprah Winfrey, J. P. Morgan, Madame C.J. Walker, Jeff Bezos, Li Ka-shing, and Mary Ellen Pleasant.

16. If you employ people in your business, pick a good day and send everyone home early if possible. Come up with innovative ways of recognizing and rewarding your employees with things like cash awards and time off awards which could be anywhere from a few hours to a full day or week. Purchase or use your computer to print "Employee of the month" certificates and present it at a company meeting. Establish a birthday club and give your employees something on their birthdays to make them feel appreciated.

17. Introduce yourself to your local bank branch managers. Know who they are because many banks

rotate mangers frequently. Ask them to explain some of the banks products that interest you. Developing and maintaining a good relationship with your bank can pay off big time down the road when you need the services of a banker, (e.g. loans for cars, boats or homes, investment advice and guidance, or start up capital for your own business).

Be creative by coming up with similar projects of your own. Once you have completed each project, please send me an email message letting me know what you gained from the experience. Or send me an email message telling me your general opinion of the book. Email me at jbrown@aboveonlymedia.com.

GIVING CREDIT WHERE CREDIT IS DUE

First, I give Almighty God the glory for giving me the inspiration and opportunity to write this book. I thank Him for giving me the diligence and perseverance needed when my financial situation seemed insurmountable. I thank God for providing me with my good health over the years, giving me the physical ability to work and earn a living. I thank Him for helping me to stay on track when I was tempted to redirect my funds foolishly on wants and desires, instead of necessities. I thank Him for opening my eyes to the truth and giving me the strength to take responsibility when I tried to blame others for my adverse financial situation. I thank God for giving me common sense, the intelligence to put my thoughts on paper, and the initiative to publish them. The title of this book was derived from two Scriptures, as follows:

*Deuteronomy 28:13 And the LORD shall make thee the head, and not the tail; and thou shalt be **above only**, and thou shalt not be beneath; if that thou hearken unto the commandments of the LORD thy God, which I command thee this day, to observe and to do them.*

*Philippians 4:6 Be **anxious for nothing**, but in everything by prayer and supplication, with thanksgiving, let your requests be made known to God; (New King James Version)*

Second, I thank my parents for setting a good example and for teaching me the value of money, conscience, personal integrity and nobility, very early in life. They showed me how and why it is important to give at every opportunity. While we did face some difficult times financially as a family, we never really suffered as so many others have. I attribute that to the diligence, persistence, and financial innovativeness of my parents when the going got rough.

Third, I wish to thank all the people who played a key role, directly or indirectly, by helping me complete this book: My family, who encouraged me to finish this project, and several close friends and coworkers who assisted with proofreading and editing. I wish to give special thanks to Sherry Hoffman-Blum of *The Word Village* in Columbia, Maryland, who was a tremendous help in providing the professional copyediting service.

Fourth, I ***thank you*** for selecting and supporting my work. I realize there are numerous documents on the same topic, and I am very grateful that you included mine. I hope it is useful to you and will continue to help you in many ways. Remember to strive for balance, save, give, insure, invest, and stay out of debt, but spend enough to enjoy your life today.

Last, but certainly not least, I want to give credit to several authors who, through their works, provided inspiration and guidance to me when I needed it. When I initially developed this book, I reversed the process that most authors use. I developed the original manuscript, then did the research to see what other authors were saying on the topic. I must have read over a hundred such books. These top ten were the ones that stood out.

One of the best sources of information in the realm of finances is Suze Orman's ***The Courage to be Rich.*** Crown Publishers Inc. This is a must have if you are serious about gaining wealth and keeping your finances together. This best-selling author is brilliant in compiling easy-to-read guidelines on creating wealth. She touches on many areas of financial aspects of life. I was fascinated at the vast amount of useful information jam packed into this book. If you are constantly on the go, try the tape series by the same name. Listen to them as you commute to/from work, as you jog, walk, or exercise. If you're smart, you will seek more of her works which were just as beneficial, ***9 Steps To Financial Freedom, You've Earned It, Don't Lose It,*** and ***The Road to Wealth***. This woman is on target.

It's About the Money by Rev. Jesse L. Jackson, Sr. and Jesse L. Jackson, Jr. with Mary Gotschall. Times Business Random House, 1999. This father and son team adds a new perspective to the world of finances. Good business sense is provided, along with spiritual advice on many topics related to building wealth.

***Blue Sky Thinking**: A Simple Yet Powerful Way To Achieve The Life You Want*, by Daniel Jingwa. BR Anchor Publishing, 1998. This outstanding work and brilliant author also gave me encouragement and inspiration to finish my book. His book provided me interesting and very effective guidelines on personal growth, achieving success, and how to deal with the day to day challenges we all face. Be sure to put this one on top of your list of resources.

The Millionaire Next Door, The Surprising Secrets of America's Wealthy, by Thomas J. Stanley, PhD, and William D. Danko, PhD. This should be required reading for anyone serious about building wealth. These two authors shatter myths and misconceptions about how we perceive the wealthy, in this amazing and highly informative book.

The Complete Book of Money Secrets, Reader's Digest Association. This book contains thousands of sound and very effective money saving tips and suggestions on many aspects of personal financial management. This advice will stand the test of time.

Multiple Streams of Income, by Robert G. Allen. This book offers timely advice and provides a splendid presentation of useful information on several income-producing strategies. This highly recommended author has done his homework. He "talks the talk" and "walks the walk." This is, in my opinion, the best of several of his successful books. He also has a comprehensive and impressive website.

Rich Dad, Poor Dad, by Robert T. Kiyosaki with Sharon L. Lechter C.P.A. This book provided me with a very interesting lesson on what the rich and wealthy teach their children about money. This one is definitely worthwhile. Also check out the version on audio cassette.

The Power of the Dime, by Bishop E. Bernard Jordan. This book provided a very impressive and useful arsenal of financial wisdom from a spiritual perspective. It is well structured, easy reading, packed with powerful tips.

All dictionary references used in ***Above Only and Anxious for Nothing*** came from the *"**WordWeb Dictionary**,"* an excellent dictionary and thesaurus software package, which provides useful features including numerous search options and customization. It interacts flawlessly with my Microsoft© Word word processing software. It was extremely helpful to me in completing my work. Check it out online by entering Wordweb into your favorite search engine.

Appendix A – BALANCE YOUR CHECKBOOK IN FIVE EASY STEPS

1. Gather your checkbook, monthly statement, cancelled checks for the period being reconciled, ATM transaction receipts, and any debit transaction receipts (from the use of check cards and debit cards).

2. During the month, as you write checks, make ATM withdrawals, or make debit transactions, you should record these in your checkbook register immediately. If you do not, now is the time to make sure all transactions are recorded. Include the date, amount, and description. Include manual and automatic deposits such as direct deposit, internet transactions, or withdrawals like automatic transfers to savings, or electronic payments of bills, etc.

3. Put the cancelled checks and deposit ticket receipts in numerical or date order. Review each one against the bank statement and against your checkbook. Confirm that the amount encoded on the bottom of the check matches what you wrote on the check and what the bank posted on your statement. When all of the above are confirmed, place a check mark next to each entry in your checkbook register and bank statement. Do the same with automatic deposits, withdrawals, and ATM receipts.

4. In your register, record any monthly fees reflected on your bank statement. Make sure they are in line with the original agreement you signed when you opened the account. Banks make mistakes too. Also, record interest payments if you have an interest bearing checking account.

5. Most banks provide a blank balance sheet with every statement. Use it to reconcile/balance your account. If they do not provide a balance sheet create one with the following: An entry for the bank "Statement Balance," a column for "Additions," a column for "Withdrawals," and an entry for the "Total."

   a. Write your current statement balance on the "Statement Balance" line.
   b. Under additions, list all deposits, transfers, and other additions to your account that you have not checked off in your register. Total the additions, add this amount to your current statement balance (line #1) and enter the total on line #2
   c. Under "withdrawals," list any checks, payments, transfers or other withdrawals that you have not checked off in your register. Total the withdrawals and enter this amount on line #3.
   d. Subtract the total withdrawals from the total additions, and enter that figure on line #4. This

amount should match your checkbook register balance.

	Additions	Withdrawals	
$_____	+_____	-_____	=_____
(1)Statement Balance	(2)Total Additions	(3)Total Withdrawals	(4)**TOTAL**

It's that simple! If the numbers don't match up, subtract the two and look for an entry equaling the difference, or review each check and deposit entry. Make sure you have recorded all ATM transactions. You may need to contact your bank if you are unable to reconcile it yourself, but you should only have to do this once. If you get into the habit of entering every transaction into your register immediately, you should not have a problem balancing in future months.

Appendix B – HOW TO READ A BASIC STOCK TICKER

Most newspapers and websites that list stock information usually provide an explanation of the symbols and data listed on the ticker. If you are a long term investor and don't feel you can take the rough ride of the daily fluctuations in stock prices, you probably shouldn't view the status every day. But whatever kind of investor you are, you need to understand the indicators. Here is a brief description with sample data, of a basic stock ticker:

STOCK	LAST	HIGH	LOW	CHG	SALES	DIV	YLD %	PE	52WK HIGH	52WK LOW
DIS	32.51	33.25	32.00	+.45	93902	.21	0.6	55	43.00	26.00
HD	52.00	52.70	51.35	+.79	60269	.16	0.3	47	60.00	34.69
CHV	95.66	95.99	94.58	+.41	16735	2.60	2.7	11	97.94	62.81

STOCK : This is the stock symbol, an acronym, abbreviation, or other representation of the company to which it refers. For example, CHV is Chevron, HD is Home Depot, DIS is Disney. Some newspapers list the company's full name.

LAST: This is the last price paid for a share of the stock when the information in the ticker was generated. For most newspapers, this would be the closing price of the day before. For most Internet quotes, this could be the last price paid that day, and could be delayed up to a specific amount of time ranging from seconds to hours. The actual price is often referred to in "points," where one point is equivalent to one dollar. If the price is shown in fractions, to get the dollar equivalent simply convert the fraction to a decimal, thus 33¼ is $33.25.

HIGH/LOW: This is the highest and lowest price paid for a share of this stock during the trading session.

CHG: This reflects the percentage of change in the stock price, up or down, from the closing price of the day before. For example, the Home Depot stock was "up" over ¾ of a point from the closing price of the day before. Simple isn't it?

SALES or VOL: This represents the number or volume of shares (times 100) traded during the session.

DIV: Dividends are the part of the earnings of a company that is paid to its investors. This reflects the amount of dividends the company paid per share, usually quarterly. Not all companies pay dividends.

YLD %: This represents the yield of the stock based on the dividend. This is the return you get on your investment, and is based on the dividend and the stock price indicated. Yield is dividend divided by the last or closing price.

P/E: This is the stock's price to earnings ratio. It is the ratio of the stock price to earnings per share. This is one of the most important factors considered when evaluating stock. It is computed by dividing the price of a share of stock by the company's annual earnings. Your broker can explain the use of this ratio in detail.

52 WK HIGH/LOW: These are the high and low prices paid per share over the last year.

Appendix C - RECOMMENDED WEB LINKS

Following, are my highly recommended Internet websites. They are jam packed with current information on many aspects of personal and business finance:

1. www.ftc.gov (Federal Trade Commission) This is my all-time favorite for financially empowering the consumer through education and information.
2. www.pueblo.gsa.gov
3. www.fool.com (The Motley Fool)
4. www.finance.yahoo.com (Yahoo)
5. www.smartmoney.com
6. www.equifax.com, www.tuc.com , and www.experian.com (The credit reporting repositories)
7. www.progressive.com, www.insweb.com, www.iquote.com, and www.quotesmith.com (Four of my favorite insurance quote service websites.)
8. www.irs.gov (Internal Revenue Service, their website is quite informative and surprisingly user friendly)
9. www.ssa.gov (Social Security Administration)
10. www.finance.yahoo.com/bp a personal bill payment site where you can pay anyone you would normally pay with a personal check. www.billingzone.com is an electronic bill presentment and payment (EBPP) solution. Businesses can use it to invoice their customers and pay their suppliers electronically.

Appendix D – SMALL BUSINESS START-UP CHECKLIST

Once you have found your niche and determined that there is a market for the type of service or product you wish to provide in your new business, there are several items to consider before developing a business plan:

___ STRUCTURE: Decide how your business will be organized: As a sole-proprietorship, partnership, corporation, non-profit organization, etc. There are specific record keeping requirements, tax liabilities, and other responsibilities for each.

___ FINANCING: Obviously you can use your own funds, or seek assistance from one of many investment and loan programs. These programs provide financing for start-up companies to help with the cost associated with getting established.

___ LICENSING: Check with your local government to determine if you must be licensed to engage in the type of business you're starting. Practically every business has some license requirement.

___ TAXES: There are state and federal regulations regarding tax obligations for business. For example, a business involving any type of in-state sales will need a permit to collect state sales tax which you will have to pay. Another example is self employment tax, it is the social security and Medicare tax for people who work for themselves, and is paid by making quarterly estimated tax payments. You are considered self-employed (and must pay this tax) if you operate a business as a sole proprietor, an independent contractor, a member of a partnership, or are otherwise in business for yourself. Even part-time work, and work done on the side (in addition to your regular job), may also be considered self-employment. Other taxes at the local level may also apply to your business.

___ ACCOUNTS: You may need to get an Employer Identification Number (EIN) from the IRS for wage reporting responsibilities. Every business will need a checking account, and to accept credit cards, you'll need a merchant account to process credit card transactions.

___ INSURANCE: Several types of insurance must be considered, including, Liability, Property, Business Interruption, "Key Man", Automobile, Officer and Director, and Home Office insurance. There are other protective considerations that may apply to your business: obtaining copyright and patents, and adhering to health and safety standards employers must follow to protect employees.

___ EQUIPMENT: Standard office equipment for any business (excluding equipment unique to your business) may include a personal computer and peripherals, fax machine, separate telephone/line, desk/chair, filing cabinet, office supplies, etc. Consider post office box service if your business is home based, and/or will receive high volumes of mail. It's secure, and provides the ability to separate business mail from personal mail.

The Small Business Administration (www.sba.gov) is the absolute best source for providing workshops and detailed information on all of these items and more. Remember, business ownership is encouraged in the United States, and there is plenty of help out there for you. The government wants us to succeed. They stand ready with resources designed to guide and assist anyone willing to learn. For example, the IRS provides a FREE small business resource guide on CD-ROM with useful information such as tax forms, instructions on how to prepare a business plan, finding financing, and more. The CD is the results of the concerted efforts of several government agencies, non-profit organizations, and educational establishments. Order CD-ROM Publication 3207 by calling (800) 829-3676, or from the IRS web site at www.irs.gov.